Locke

THE MANKIND SERIES OF GREAT ADVENTURES OF HISTORY

THE HUMAN SIDE OF HISTORY

THE MANKIND SERIES OF GREAT ADVENTURES OF HISTORY

THE HUMAN SIDE OF HISTORY
MAN'S MANNERS, MORALS AND GAMES

Compiled, edited and with an Introduction
by Raymond Friday Locke

A Mankind   *Book*

MANKIND PUBLISHING COMPANY
LOS ANGELES

Library of Congress Catalog Card Number: 70-135909
SBN: 87687-004-3

Book design by Andrew Furr
© 1970 by Mankind Publishing Company, 8060 Melrose Avenue, Los Angeles, California. All rights reserved.

CONTENTS

INTRODUCTION

The history of man involves more than the study of battles won and lost, and the ever-changing boundaries of countries. The real history lies within man himself. Certainly the study of political and military history are important but they are no less important than social history. Too often the social, or human side of man's history is neglected. When we read of one of Alexander the Great's military victories we should like to know more than the date of the battle and how many men were lost. It would be interesting to know how the common soldier felt about the battle, how his wounds were treated, what medicines he took for his illnesses and how he amused himself in his leisure time. We also might ask how his wife did her laundry and what cosmetics she wore!

This human side of history can often be more fascinating than, say, Napoleonic campaigns. This unique collection of articles on man's manners, morals and games is not only informative, it is often marvelously fun. Included in the collection is a survey of the first 100 years of college football, a history of golf, cosmetics, ice cream, coffee, glass, valentines, baby nursers, and television. On the more serious side there is an interesting new look at the Victorians, and studies of juvenile delinquency, prehistoric diseases and primitive medicine and the effects of the deadly Black Plague on a dark, superstitious world. I hope it includes a few items that you never thought of as being "history."

RAYMOND FRIDAY LOCKE
Editor, Mankind Magazine

Detail from a Greek vase, approximately twenty-five hundred years old, showing Achilles and Ajax, as soldiers in the field, playing an ancient version of chess

THE PAST
IS PROLOGUE

by Sam Elkin

*S*hakespeare is making a comment on mankind's social history when Antonio says in *The Tempest*— ". . . what's past is prologue . . ." Today, carved into stone on the Archives Building in Washington, D.C., we can read a shortened version of Shakespeare's line: Past Is Prologue.

At first glance the phrase appears to be a contradiction, especially when the meaning of prologue is defined as an "introduction," a "preliminary," a "preface" to a "poem, novel, or play." With this definition we can generalize by saying past is beginning. But that threatens to turn the phrase into something worse than a mere contradiction—the confusion of a deliberate paradox which seems absurd.

However, it would be absurd to deny the remark Thomas Carlyle made in 1840 that "The Present is the living sum-total of the whole Past." For when we examine the past under the penetrating light of mankind's social history the phrase suddenly blooms into a tough and durable truth. What becomes obvious is that men concerned about mankind in every age have acknowledged the debt man owes to both past man and future man.

"Study the past, if you would divine the future," advised Confucius around 500 B.C., and in 1775 Patrick Henry said, "I know no way of judging the future but by the past." In 1821 Lord Byron echoed the thought with "The best prophet of the future is the past," while Albert Einstein phrased the idea in more personal language when he wrote in 1930, "A hundred times every day I remind myself that my inner and outer life are based on the labors of other men, living and dead."

Modern man, if he is to understand the world in which he lives *now*, must recognize that the present is one unbroken line between the past and the future. This is the truth in Past Is Prologue.

Evidence of this truth is everywhere around us today in our daily lives—even in something so insignificant as a joke. A customer enters a barber shop and is immediately approached by a barber who asks him how he wants his hair cut. Replies the customer: "In silence."

That Joe Miller, a popular English comedian playing the London Drury Lane circuit back in the early 1700's, probably delighted audiences with this joke is not the point. More pertinent is the question: How old is the joke?

In a book titled *A Day In Old Athens* written by William Stearns Davis and copyrighted in 1914, there is the following interesting bit of information about ancient Athenian life.

"How shall I cut your hair, sir?" once asked the court tonsor of King Archelaus of Macedon.

"In silence," came the grim answer.

"How shall I cut your hair, sir?" asked the court tonsor
of King Archelaus, father of Philip of Macedon (above).
"In silence," came the grim reply.

Davis introduces the joke by emphasizing that "the garrulity of barbers is already proverbial," and the date, he points out in a preface, is 360 B.C.

More fascinating than the joke is our knowledge today that barbering was already an old profession 400 years before Christ was born. And the whole truth is even more startling.

Today's barber might sing the praises of his straight-edged razor as it glides over a customer's face. Indeed, in our commercialized world he might sing louder over his modern day steel and superior honing process. But in fact, today's straight-edged razor is only a slight improvement in design and quality to a slate-handled obsidian blade men were using some 6000 years ago.

Similarly, if today's gourmet swoons at the taste of some delicious golden fried food, he might easily be revived by the fact that thousands of years ago in a land known by the lovely name of Mesopotamia (Iraq today), mothers were frying foods for their families in pans very much like the frying pan used in today's kitchen.

The social history of mankind which is the history of man's customs, manners, thoughts, ambitions, and artifacts is full of surprises for modern man. In our world where things too easily assume the status of symbols it is a simple matter to lose sight of the fact that what we consider to be relatively modern inventions are often only improvements on a remarkable number of tools ancient man produced with a high degree of skill.

For example we date the invention of the dry cell battery to Allesandro Volta (1745-1827), the Italian physicist from whom, in fact, comes our present day word *volt*. But in Baghdad today there exists unmistakable evidence that a version of this battery was being used by men who lived in Persia during the Sassanid Dynasty—and that dynasty is dated from 226 to 640 A.D.

Today's do-it-yourselfer, armed with his arsenal of mechanized tools, would be in for a shock if he considered the Egyptian carpenter of 4500 years ago. According to *Everyday Life In Ancient Times*, published by the National Geographic Society, an XIth Dynasty (Middle Kingdom) carpenter was gluing six different kinds of wood together—willow, fig, acacia, sycamore, cedar, and tamarisk—thereby inventing plywood. He was using wooden pegs for nails. He was able to give wood surfaces a smooth, even finish; he understood the uses of coarse crack-fillers; and his glue was very much like the modern day carpenter's glue. "His bronze cutting and boring tools—saw, adze, chisel, knife, scraper, and bow drill—were equipped with hardwood handles," and "his mallet and square were of hardwood, and his whetstone usually of quartzite."

The Egyptian woodworker of 2500 B.C. was a master craftsman, and much of what he left us of his tools and furniture exists to this very day. More imposing even than his tools is the fact that he was familiar with "most of the (carpentry) devices known to the modern cabinetmaker," the pegged tenon and overlapped mitre joints as well as the "various rabbet, dado and lap joints, and the dovetail."

And what is probably the most startling piece of information for today's weekend carpenter comes from *The Origin Of Things*, in which Dr. Julius E. Lips writes, "Many ancient tools have not only remained unsurpassed by modern man, but the original good design has in some cases actually deteriorated or been forgotten during the ages."

The point is not that there is very little new under the sun, but that "there is nothing new except what has been forgotten." Louis Pauwels and Jacques Bergier, in their book *The Morning Of The Magicians*, attribute this remark to Marie Antoinette while she was touching up an ancient hat. More than a beauty and fashion note, it should serve to remind us in our time that past is prologue in just about every walk of life.

When Iran was the world's first great empire around 500 B.C., Iranian doctors were the forerunners of this century's old-fashioned general practitioner. According to Bart Winer's *Life In The Ancient World,* Iranian doctors traveled from town to town on horseback. "When attending a patient, the doctor wore a cloth over his head to keep his breath from contaminating anything." Perhaps that ancient healer did not know precisely why he covered his face with what looked like the surgeon's mask of today, but the fact that he did indicates he suspected an unseen world of disease carriers—and that suspicion was enough when Louis Pasteur came on the scene nearly 25 centuries later.

In Mesopotamia when a man and woman wished to marry they signed a marriage contract by rolling their fingernails over wet clay. True, it took a few thousand years for the idea to develop in the mind of man, but when it did he turned his finger around to discover the most widely accepted system of individual identification in use today.

In such bits of social history we have clear-cut examples of past is prologue. To list others equally fascinating we must enter a field of science that, historically, is hardly more than a hundred years old. Alexander Pope said: "The proper study of mankind is man." We might say that the proper study of mankind's social history is archaeology.

Deriving from two Greek words—*arche* meaning origin or beginning and *ology* meaning study or knowledge—the science of archaeology is a way of looking into the past in order to understand what we have in the present so that we can improve what we leave for the future.

Ever since Heinrich Schliemann, the man who uncovered Homer's fabled city of Troy around 1870, ar-

Etruscan vase painting showing a Dionysiac situation

chaeologists have developed a science out of digging, recording, tracing, deciphering, and reconstructing the artifacts of man as they existed long ago. Like a detective the archaeologist bridges thousands of years into the past for us so that we become eyewitnesses to past man.

Thousands of years from today future man will have less trouble understanding exactly what took place, for example, during World War II. At his fingertips will be the millions of words written and preserved on microfilm. There will be countless photographs to scrutinize, huge stocks of motion pictures to examine, recorded voices and sounds to hear.

But the study of past man unfortunately cannot be investigated in the same way future man will explore present man. Past man could only leave for the future his writings, his word-of-mouth stories, his paintings, his sculpture. As communication methods these were effective. But all of them were and still are at the mercy of accidents, weather, decay, and misunderstanding.

It is remarkable that today we know as much as we do about the past. By digging up and studying the bits and pieces of things ancient man fought with, built with, played with, grew, ate and manufactured; by translating the written stories, laws, religions, and business contracts in his daily life; and by reconstructing the toys, musical instruments, paintings on walls, pottery, sculpture, and cloth ancient man created, archaeology has uncovered an astonishing amount of information about man's beginnings.

We know that around 500 B.C. Iranian men rode on horses and played a game with a bat and a ball that is very much like the game of polo played today. We have unmistakable evidence in our museums that boys spun tops, played dice and checkers, threw the discus, boxed, and even carried pocket knives thousands of years ago.

We know that certain words we speak and write—chicory, crocus, myrrh and saffron, to name only a few—are the very same words spoken and written by Mesopotamians who also invented the wheel, writing, law, and codes of behavior still in existence to this very day.

We are, in fact, familiar with the trial of a Mesopotamian by the name of Kushshiharbe. He was the chief magistrate of Nuzi, a city in Iraq which lies ten miles southeast of the modern oil center of Kirkuk. Nearly 3500 years ago Kushshiharbe was found guilty of corruption. We even know that his accuser was one of his former henchmen turned state's witness.

We have today in our possession the very items used by the Egyptian Princess Sit-Hathor-Yunet, daughter of King Se'-Worset II, as she sat at her dressing table in 1900 B.C. With a little imagination we can see her "make up" her face with rouge that lies in a silver dish, "make up" her eyes with a black cosmetic which she applies with a slender ebony stick. We can watch her examine the result in a small, round, silver mirror which has a handle made of polished volcanic glass.

We know today that a race of people called Sumerians invented the 60 minute hour, that 2500 years B.C. the Cretans had a sewerage system about as good as ours is today, that the Egyptians played handball very much as it is played today—except that the ball they used was made of bran, or husks of grain, and covered with leather.

We know that wealthy Romans in the time of Julius Caesar, only a few years as time goes before the birth of Christ, banqueted on cold wild boar surrounded by all kinds of pickled vegetables; oysters, shellfish, a relish made of fish, wine, vinegar and wild pepper, each of the ingredients coming from a different part of the then known world; wild fowl served with grain; liver of a white goose fattened on ripe figs, shoulder of hare,

17

broiled blackbirds; bright red apples, and black mulberries plucked before the sun was high.

Because of the science of archaeology we have in existence today excellent copies of an essay schoolboys in ancient Egypt wrote in their classrooms as a prescribed lesson just as schoolboys of today do in their classrooms. These copies, written on papyrus paper, were buried in tombs and left in Egyptian classrooms to be covered by dust and earth and the decay of a crumbling civilization.

The lesson told about an Egyptian father who advised his son to become a writer because in his opinion it was the best of trades for any man. After vividly describing to his son all the miserable, back-breaking, poor-paying jobs of the metalworker and the carpenter, of the embalmer and the barber, of the disease-ridden perils faced by the traveling merchant and the dangers lying in wait for couriers (postmen) from barbarians and lions, the father concluded his lecture with: "Only a scribe is his own boss!"

Today we have so much detailed information about past man that if we wish to go back 5000 years to watch the ancient Egyptian making beer we can enter a brewery which, in those days, was almost as important as the granary or the bakery.

First we should know that to the Egyptian of 3000 B.C. beer was not only a pleasure drink, it was an important food item in his daily diet. It also played an important part in his religious life. Isis, ancient Egyptian goddess of nature, was supposed to have introduced beer to the Egyptians.

Inside the brewery, which is a small room with a door but no windows, we see the barley or wheat brought to a man who cracks it in a stone mortar. To crack the grain the man is using what resembles a huge baseball bat.

The cracked grain is then placed in a limestone mill

18

which looks like a narrow horse trough. A woman, and this job is always performed by a woman, now grinds the grain into flour. From her the flour is passed on to a man working at a kneading tray. By adding to the flour a yeasty residue of just baked bread, the man molds the dough into loaves which he places on a low stove.

After the loaves are fully risen they are crumbled and mixed with a large quantity of water. This mixture is dumped into tall, wide-mouthed jars. Then a man begins the mixing process by mashing it with his feet like the squashing of grapes.

This mash is allowed to ferment for a day or two. What's left is a thick, lumpy liquid. This is strained through a sieve and poured into a brewer's vat which looks like one of the mashing jars but is reinforced by a stand on the bottom and what resembles a tray over the mouth. There is a short-nosed snout on the vat, out of which flows a liquid white in color, foaming, and slightly sourish in odor. This is the beer drained off the top while the dregs drop to the bottom of the vat. It is poured into pottery jars which are immediately covered with cones made from mud of the Nile.

Sometimes the mixture is sweetened with dates or spiced with various herbs. Beer destined for royalty, nobles, and officials is put through a refinishing process. Beer for peasants and laborers contains the hulls of various cereals used.

Today Egyptian beer resembles ancient Egyptian beer in its thinness. But then malt was unknown and today's Egyptian wheat beer has about a seven percent alcoholic content. Interestingly enough, the word for today's beer is *booza*, and in the Hungarian language the word *booza* means wheat.

This is but one more example of our ubiquitous past is prologue. Through language and custom, through the social history of mankind, the phrase illuminates an interdependence of life that stretches back to the beginning of time and goes on into a future we cannot possibly envision.

The foundation upon which the past is prologue is archaeology, the great master key that opens long sealed tombs. From ancient ruins the archaeologist removes anything that will help him pierce the darkness of a buried civilization covered by the litter and dust of time. All his digging, his fitting of stone to stone, his cataloguing of arrowheads, vases, works of art, his reconstruction of *things*, is important.

If the piecing together and the listings of *things* were all we could expect from the archaeologist, then his discoveries of new ancient cities would hardly cause a ripple of excitement. What clutches our imagination when the ruins of an ancient city are uncovered is that we are opening still another door to the mystery of man.

In a very real sense we are able to stand at the elbow of the archaeologist while he digs and reconstructs his finds. Then when he analyzes those finds, interprets them for us, gives them meaning in personal terms—only then can most of us begin to have that fascinating peek into mankind.

As the archaeologist unfolds ancient man's daily life for us, that time and place loses its mystery and we are transported into the past. It is almost as if our buried ancestor rises from the dead to take our hand and whisper in our ear: "Come with me as I walk through my city. Stay with me as I eat my meals and work at my job. Let me take you home to greet my wife and speak to my children. I will open your eyes and help you understand how you became what you are today."

And so in the time of Nebuchadnezzar's Babylonia (605-562 B.C.), H.W.F. Saggs, in *Everyday Life In Babylonia & Assyria*, follows a mythical Bel-ibni through a workday rather typical of the time.

"Bel-ibni and his wife" wake in their home "just be-

Ancient Greek shaving scene

fore dawn," kiss "each other and the children," and then the master of the house enters his bath where he washes himself with "a kind of soap made of ashes of certain plants mixed with fats."

After a substantial breakfast, Bel-ibni goes off to "work at his workshop in the goldsmiths' bazaar." There, with his older son helping him, they convert plain gold "castings into fine examples of Babylonian embossed and engraved ornamentation and filigree work." Then it is midday and time for lunch. Back at the house a light lunch is waiting, after which Bel-ibni and his wife retire to their bedroom for a nap.

They awake refreshed and make love. "This (is) not only a pleasure but also a positive duty. Bel-ibni's wife (is) five months pregnant, and the omen collections stated that this (is) a highly favorable time for this activity." After Bel-ibni takes another bath, he and his son return "for further work in the goldsmiths' bazaar" where they stay until dusk. Then back home for "the main evening meal."

H.W.F. Saggs then describes a minor festival taking place at the local temple that night, to which Bel-ibni and his family go. Among friends and neighbors in the "temple courtyard," lit by flickering "torches made of reeds soaked in crude bitumen," there is "dancing and singing." Finally, it is time to go home again.

Just before retiring, Bel-ibni watches his daughter and sons play "at a kind of draughts," and after a light snack "the day (comes) to an end."

Thus, a day in the life of a family 2500 years ago becomes almost a carbon copy of family life in the twentieth century. In that fact lies archaeology's great fascination. We can all be awed by the massive mystery of a pyramid, but when the archaeologist digs out of the earth a baby's nursing bottle thousands of years old we are suddenly startled by the realization that very little is really new.

Archaeology forces us into the understanding that life has been, is, and will always be one continuous flow of ideas and customs and legends from men in the past to men in the present to men beyond into the future. And in revealing what it was men once lived for and died for we are also being told something vital and crucial about our own lives in our own time.

This is what Albert Einstein meant when he said that his "inner and outer life are based on the labors of other men, living and dead." This is precisely what other great men of the past have readily acknowledged. Columbus openly admitted his debt to old philosophers and poets. Galileo made it quite clear that his ideas came from ancient science.

Copernicus wrote Pope Paul III that his reading of ancient authors reinforced his ideas on the movement of the earth. Isaac Newton said, "If I have seen further it is by standing on the shoulders of giants." And Albert Einstein put the same thought this way: "I have stood upon the shoulders of men in the past, and thus was able to look over the wall.

"Bear in mind that the wonderful things you learn in your schools are the work of many generations, produced by enthusiastic effort and infinite labor in every country of the world. All this is put into your hands as your inheritance in order that you may receive it, honor it, add to it, and one day faithfully hand it on to your children. Thus do we mortals achieve immortality in the permanent things which we create in common. If you always keep that in mind you will find a meaning in life and work and acquire the right attitude toward other nations and ages."

H. T. Wells' painting of Victoria greeted as Queen

THE VICTORIANS REVISITED

by Gerald Carson

*T*hings are looking up for the Victorians. A generation ago, these respectable, bearded gentlemen and hoop-skirted women were commonly regarded with amusement or outright disapproval because of their formal manners, their concern for appearance rather than substance, their pretentious life-style, their sentimentality, their stuffy taste in the arts. Now distance lends enchantment. Even the recollection of the marbleized virtues of the period has been modified by a stream of biographies, memoirs, and underground novels which demonstrate that many of the Victorians were really quite wicked. So we think better of them. Even the cast-iron deer on the lawn, the black walnut and horse-hair furniture, the cluttered parlor, the tassels and fringe, the determination of the Victorians to exhaust the technical possibilities of the jigsaw—

all of these expressions of nineteenth-century civilization now seem a charming background for feminine figures strolling on the croquet courts with flirty fans and tiny parasols.

In speaking of the Victorian Age, or in giving any period a name, one should always bear in mind that such descriptive terms are no more than a kind of shorthand, useful to historians who like to deal in neat categories. Such limiting adjectives as "Victorian" or "Edwardian" or whatever do no harm so long as we do not apply them too rigorously. There is, of course, in every time period an indwelling spirit, something in the social atmosphere like an airborne yeast, which gives that moment in history its special character. And we find authentic character in Victoria, a good, Christian woman with appealing domestic tastes, who sang Mozart after supper with her beloved Albert and went to bed at half-past ten.

Since Queen Victoria reigned from 1837 to 1901, what we are looking at is actually the major portion of the nineteenth century, a time of extraordinary scientific, social, and technological advancement. But the term "Victorian" is usually applied not to a whole civilization but to the sensibilities and moral outlook of a vigorous, new middle class, and the artistic and decorative motifs which it responded to. And most particularly, "Victorian" was a synonym for a strict code of sexual behavior.

Here in America we still use the adjective as freely as do the English and in each country it has the same connotations. It seems strange at first glance to speak of *American* Victorian since Victoria was never our queen.

Yet the only queen whose name we invoke in the United States is Victoria. The reasons for this include such elements as England's power and prestige a hundred years ago, the redoubtable personality of Victoria herself, and perhaps when we borrowed the word a streak of colonial deference still existed in the American psyche. But the most compelling reason of all lies, I think, in the fact that the British monarchy provided the entourage of a royal court which set values and codified social institutions. Democracy offered no such guide. Certainly no descriptive phrase ever came out of Washington or any phase of our national life to type a period as does the name of the Widow of Windsor.

For Americans, the nineteenth century was a time of optimism and energetic expansion. New men pushed forward aggressively, backed by new fortunes made in coal, steel, oil, railroads, cut whiskey, war contracts, and stock speculation. There were, in consequence of this social mobility, congressmen who tried to eat the doilies, captains of industry who drank the lemon water from the finger bowls, wives who addressed their husband as "my duck."

Refinement and coarseness were mingled together, while the grip of orthodox Calvinism remained so firm that when Fredrika Bremer, the Swedish novelist, approached the piano to demonstrate a point about Swedish music, Mr. Emerson forbade it: "No, Miss Bremer, this is Massachusetts, and Sunday evening! I can't have it!"

The same Sabbatarian neopuritanism prevailed in England. At about the same time that Emerson spoke out in such alarm, Lord Cardigan was reprimanded for flogging a soldier of the 11th Hussars. Why? Because the whipping took place on a Sunday, during the hour for church service.

Let us not underestimate the zest for life of these sturdy Victorians. The English tucked their napkins inside their collars and stowed away gargantuan meals. They climbed the world's most challenging mountains for sport, industrialized their society, produced a formidable new middle class. At the great exposition at London's Crystal Palace in 1851, they generously admired such evidences of American accomplishment as the Mc-Cormick reaper and the Colt revolver. Yet the level of taste was such that they were also delighted by a grotesque result of the taxidermist's art—an exhibit of stuffed cats sitting on chairs and taking tea.

The High Victorians in America shared similar tastes and manners, while launching the greatest period of reform ever seen in this country, touching such diverse areas as food, diet and health, the legal status of women, and the protection of children. They agitated for the ten-hour day, the improvement of prisons and asylums. They improved education, founded the American Red Cross, introduced a new concept of mercy in the treatment of animals, supported the temperance and peace movements. Topping all this, they made the climactic effort to abolish human slavery, and paid the necessary price to do it.

Yet, at the same time, and this is confusing to us today, they accepted misery and poverty as a necessary and permanent condition of society and shared fully the materialistic ethic of the Reverend Russell Herman Conwell, popular lecturer and pastor, who thundered from pulpit and platform, "You should be a righteous man, and if you were you would be rich."

Distinctions of dress, education, class, and family inherited from the previous century were blurred or pushed aside by the new plutocracy. But there remained a gnawing anxiety about the social graces and about the questions of taste.

There was wide agreement that good taste was important. But what was it? At the great exposition held in Philadelphia in 1876 to celebrate one hundred years of American Independence, good taste was equated with ostentation, as visitors to the fair gazed upon heavily ornamented suites of furniture embellished with griffins and cornices, claw feet and spindles, combining all materials and textures. The designers floundered, sought inspiration in seventeenth-century Flanders, retreated into monasticism with William Morris and sighed with the maidens in the fluttering draperies of Gilbert and Sullivan's "Patience"—"Oh to be Early English ere it is too late."

Perhaps the social change with the greatest impact upon the century was the shift in the position of women. The woman of the eighteenth century was a full partner with her husband. This was equally true whether she was chatelaine of a Virginia plantation or stood beside her husband with gun and hoe in the equalitarianism of the pioneer West.

But in the nineteenth century with the growth of cities, increased dispersion of wealth, and the arrival on our shores of cheap domestic labor, the woman who lived in some economic comfort literally lost her job. So she fell back in frustration upon charitable work, hemming napkins or doing fancy work for church fairs, packing barrels for the foreign missions, fabricating homey articles which no one wanted—pen wipers, covers for perfume bottles, crazy quilts, and wax flowers. This still left ample time for fierce social competition and such other spheres of activity as were thought suitable for a lady. But they were severely limited.

Mrs. William Appleton of Boston, for example, a pioneer leader in the cause of animal welfare, could not sit on the board of the Massachusetts Society for the Prevention of Cruelty to Animals because she was a woman. This omission, I am happy to say, was ultimately remedied when a change in the climate of opinion permitted the use of her name.

Housework was done by a staff which was numerous but poorly paid. The skills of these domestics may be inferred from the experience of a New York matron living on Gramercy Park, who after a vigorous session with her latest jewel, a Finnish girl, finally burst out in exasperation: "You can't cook, you can't make beds, you can't sweep, you don't even open the door for visitors. Is there anything on God's earth that you can do?"

"Yes, ma'am," the Finn replied. "I can milk reindeer."

If a Victorian girl didn't make it to the altar, she could teach school or become a missionary. She might attempt to write if her work promoted the notion of feminine submissiveness and fragility. A touch of tuberculosis in a heroine was deemed irresistible.

But not all the women of the epoch were willing to live and die as Whistler's-mother types. The business girl appeared on the Washington scene during the manpower shortage of the Civil War years. The invention of the typewriter placed women alongside men in the business office of the eighties and the telephone introduced the switchboard girl known as "Central," who probably did more for the promotion of public courtesy than has any other figure in our national life.

The anxieties of a new public deeply concerned about the proprieties produced a steady flow of books dealing with etiquette and conduct. The middle-class matron, lately arrived to her responsible position, and desiring to conform to the pattern followed by those placed just above her, felt the need of a passport to culture and the polite norms of behavior.

Many hack writers were available to meet the demand. They stuffed their works with an odd mixture of snobbery and genuinely good counsel, borrowing shamelessly from each other, even lifting material from similar publications in England without troubling themselves to change a reference from Regent's Park to Central Park, or editing out an expression foreign to American speech, such as "linen draper," or eliminating useless information, such as how to address a letter to a duke.

This sub-literature became so remunerative that it

attracted "name" authors. Among them were Catherine Maria Sedgwick of the illustrious Stockbridge, Massachusetts, family, and Mrs. Lydia H. Sigourney, once known as "the most famous of the female bards of her country." Mrs. Sarah Madeleine Vinton Dahlgren, Washington hostess and widow of an admiral, and Mrs. Mary Elizabeth Sherwood, another social leader in Washington, were among the counselors who addressed themselves to the problems of those who felt at a disadvantage in the social scramble.

Two of the Reverend Lyman Beecher's gifted daughters, Catherine and Harriet Beecher Stowe, wrote on decorum and deportment, while other practitioners retired coyly behind such pseudonyms as "Count D'Orsay," the name of a famous French dandy, the "Marquise de Fontenay," or just plain, sensible "Aunt Matilda."

The handbooks on correct manners were frankly addressed to the unshaped and uncombed. The title page of one such work indicates the ground these volumes attempted to cover: "The lady's guide to perfect gentility, in manners, dress, and conversation, in the family, in company, at the pianoforte, the table, in the street, and in gentlemen's society. Also a useful instructor in letter writing, toilet preparations, fancy needlework, millinery, dress-making, care of the wardrobe, the hair, teeth, hands, lips, complexion, etc."

The writers on refined manners passed down the word of new developments in the higher levels of society. If the pewter-and-pressed-glass caster in the center of the family dining-room table was no longer in fashion, they said so; or they tipped off their readers to the social dictate that every family with any pretense to culture should own a canary. Most revealing of all the material in these books on how to behave are the caveats, the negative rules. For the warnings portray what people actually did, the reality rather than the

31

fantasy.

Here are a few instances: gentlemen do not anchor their napkins through a buttonhole, wave their knives and forks, or cool their coffee in their saucers. They chat pleasantly at the table and make witty remarks. But not too witty. They never swear, nor do ladies use the feminine substitutes for profanity, such as "the dickens." When a gentleman greets a lady of his acquaintance on the street he always removes his derby from his head and his cigar from his mouth. Should he use an indelicate word or expression, not the shadow of a smile shall flit across the lady's face: she will not understand.

Judging by the extended treatment given the topic, one of the great difficulties of social intercourse during the Red Plush Era was how to carry on a conversation. Here are a few of the guidelines offered and I believe we can agree that they are well founded on experience and are applicable to all times and places:

Don't make a display of your knowledge of foreign languages or of technical terms in general society. Do not talk shop. Avoid long, tiresome anecdotes. On the otherhand, when someone starts to tell a story you know, let him finish rather than cut him down with, "Yes, I know that story." Puns and gossip are off limits, as well as politics and religion. Be considerate. Be tolerant. Remember that triviality comes naturally from trivial people. Contribute your fair share of the talk, but never let your supply of conversation exceed the demand. Help others to be pleased with themselves.

A man should speak to a pretty woman of the beauties of her mind, not her face, for, says the astute author of the *Art of Conversing*, published in Boston in 1846: "If she is pretty, she already knows it." When the family dines alone and the children are at the table, the parents select the subject of conversation, the young members occasionally being permitted to make contributions of moderate length, expressed in quiet tones. Shall we pause here for a moment of silent reflection?

Recurring themes include the etiquette of mourning which at least one author hinted, with unusual candor, often grew more elaborate and costly in inverse ratio to the actual grief felt by the bereaved. There was instruction in how to write letters to meet various standard situations, how to shake hands, and advice upon such down-to-earth matters as spitting, bathing, and eating corn on the cob. A whole chapter was commonly required to do justice to the niceties of the social call and the formalities connected with the white blizzard of visiting cards which descended into the silver card-receiver in the front hall.

The extreme of punctilio in this matter was reached when Miss Ellen Harvie of Frankfort, Kentucky, was walking along the street one day and saw that Mrs. Watson's chimney was on fire. Miss Ellen's first impulse was to rush to notify her friend. Then she recollected that Mrs. Watson had owed her a return call for some time. So with genuine regret she continued on her way.

The prudery, the little snobberies, the excessive regard felt for a collection of rules and shibboleths which one finds in the literature of manners, have moved later and more informal generations to laughter and parody. After due allowance is made for other times, other circumstances, it is doubtless true that these arbiters consulted in secret by the Victorians provided good mortar for binding the social structure together. And we must not suppose that the need for guidance in the social forms is a thing of the past. Otherwise, how can we account for the fact that everybody knows the names of Emily Post and Amy Vanderbilt?

One suspects that the ultra-refinement of the Victorians was not very deep-seated since excessive delicacy may indicate an underlying grossness. Mrs. Frances

Trollope, the English novelist who published rather spiteful comments on the folkways of Americans, observed that the American ladies could always understand words with a double meaning. Yet she was informed that in the United States it was considered quite shocking for men and women to sit together on the grass at a picnic.

A willingness to tamper with the integrity of art—in the service of a higher cause, of course—is represented in the activities of a New England reverend named William L. Gage. Gage, who was an American version of that Dr. Thomas Bowdler of Edinburgh who de-sexed Shakespeare in ten volumes, presented readings from Shakespeare which, according to his announcements, had been Hollanderized to remove what he termed the blemishes of a less genteel age.

A similar celebrated instance of the same point of view occurred when Mrs. Nathaniel Hawthorne worked over her husband's notebooks after his death, modifying or eliminating words and passages which did not fit her conception of elegance or propriety.

Examples of this ascetic culture could be multiplied almost without end. The Reverend Cornelius B. Smith, Rector of St. James' Church in New York City, could enjoy Shakespeare's comedies with a clear conscience when Mr. and Mrs. William Hunter Kendall, a popular English acting team, played opposite each other. Since they were husband and wife, what was called the "embarrassment" of the courting scenes was avoided.

Edward Everett, Unitarian minister, teacher, orator, and governor of Massachusetts, draped his copy of the Apollo Belvidere with a sheet; while Captain Frederick Marryat, the English novelist, noticed a square piano at a young ladies' seminary in New York State with its legs, or rather, its limbs, encased in little, frilly pantalets.

So much titillation was extracted by the public from

Hiram Powers' nude statue, "The Greek Slave," in which observers found a pleasing combination of the idealistic and the carnal, that in Cincinnati the unclothed body was dressed in a calico blouse and flannel drawers. Powers, the leading native American sculptor, had trouble in Boston, too. When his "Chanting Cherubs" was exhibited there, it was necessary to put pants on the cherubs, the same treatment accorded a live orangutang which was making appearances in the city at about the same time.

Not all of the American Victorians were refined or sentimental. A raucous best-seller of the period was *Peck's Bad Boy and His Pa;* also *The Groceryman and Peck's Bad Boy.* Both books were filled with sadistic pranks and mocking laughter. The popularity of Judge George W. Peck's writings is a significant indicator of the rebellion of a minority which relished hits aimed at such sacred targets as family, church, and business.

In Mark Twain, too, we see the obverse side of Victorian blandness. One literary project which he began but did not complete burlesqued the etiquette books. He suggested, for example, to those attending a funeral, "Do not criticize the person in whose honor the entertainment is given. . . . If the odor of flowers is too oppressive for your comfort, remember that they were not brought there for you, and that the person for whom they were brought suffers no inconvenience from their presence."

Some Victorians, then, it is well to recall, took a disenchanted view of the foibles of their contemporaries and understood the cleansing power of laughter.

Another touchstone of the period was the wide use of the biological word "female" to denote a woman. Margaret Fuller loathed the word. And in England Jane Austen had the forward-looking Elizabeth Bennett in *Pride and Prejudice* say, "Do not consider me as an elegant female . . . but as a rational creature." Women who were too assertive or "dashing" were said to be guilty of something called "female indelicacy," while all the ills of the flesh is heir to were gathered together in the advertising of patent medicines, under the catch phrase "female weakness."

The objection to the word was that a female was not necessarily a woman and it seemed to be slyly erotic and to set women apart as being in some way less than human. Mrs. Sarah Joseph Hale, editor of *Godey's Lady's Book*, and a notable career woman, carried on such a vigorous campaign against the word that when her friend, Matthew Vassar, founder of Vassar Female College, wrote to her on the letterhead of the College, he always drew a line through the second word.

The Poughkeepsie, New York, philanthropist was happy when he could report to Mrs. Hale that the stone bearing the offensive word had been removed from the facade of the main college building. A bricked over blank space is still visible there, to perplex the uninitiated visitor. A later Vassar poet—*not* Edna St. Vincent Millay—has celebrated this event in singing:

> "They took the 'Female'
> off the spoons
> As well as off the College."

We must give the Victorians high marks for the zest and ingenuity they displayed in the area of do-it-yourself entertainment. They were devoted to music, especially to songs and ballads likely to bring on a good cry. Typical titles are "Whisper Softly, Mother's Dying," "The Letter Edged in Black," and parlor pieces like "Hearts and Flowers," all rendered on the rosewood piano while the gas jet hissed a soft obligato.

Through ownership of a piano, families of median social position were able to put their claims to gentility on display. Little daughters were sent to the music teacher to learn to punch out Shubert's "March Militaire" under a framed print of the Parthenon or Rosa

VICTORIAN ART

Art, it has been said, reflects the times. Certainly Victorian art reflected the times as it was most often precious, sometimes poignant, and almost always pastoral. The portfolio that follows, all from decade between 1888 and 1898, is typical. Below is Mlle E. Gardner's Truants *(1892).*

Spring *by F. Lamy, 1892*

The Washerwomen *by L. A. Lhermitte, 1898*

The Rest *by L.A. Lhermitte, 1888*

Bonheur's "The Horse Fair." As early as the decade of the 1860's, pianos were selling at the rate of 25,000 a year and by the end of the century there were a million instruments in American homes.

Naturally, then, the literature of deportment had something to say to amateur performers and their audiences. The listener, at a party where music was introduced, was urged to pay attention under the threat of an embarrassment related by Mrs. Stowe. On one occasion when the music suddenly dropped to a pianissimo, a voice rose above the music, saying: "I always cook mine in vinegar." Do not take your music roll with you when invited to an affair at a private home, one mentor warned, as a hint you expect to be asked to perform. If there is a request, wait for a seconder. If it is your unalterable intention to sing or play, then do it. But do not hang back to be coaxed. Lady singers should not offer songs descriptive of masculine passion. Pianists should not disparage the instrument which is available. It was also suggested that a short piece would always be a happy choice and the artiste was reminded to receive any acclaim with modesty since the applause may not have been for the performance but for its conclusion.

Other popular forms of self-entertainment in the mid-century included charades, monologues, and recitations. A universal drill in the elementary schools required the scholars to memorize and recite "pieces." They were carefully selected examples of poetry or prose whose literary merit and moral precepts rendered them suitable for public performance or private enjoyment. This taste for rhetoric and forensics was part of a national preoccupation with eloquence, or at least elocution.

The dramatic gestures taught by Francois Delsarte were widely admired and taught. They served to illustrate such ideas as "Remorse," "Accusation," "Joy,"

"Disdain." The position for "Repulse" was assumed for the delivery of such a line as "Avaunt! Richard's himself again." The position called "Discerning"—with hand over the eyes peering—was taken when the speaker declaimed, "Land, ho! cried the man at the masthead."

Most Americans who are now members of the Social Security set can still recall fragments and tag-ends from this elocutionary discipline: "The Assyrian came down like a wolf on the fold"; "'Tis Christmas Day in the workhouse . . ."; or, "Father, dear Father, come home with me now!" Shy country boys learned to mount the platform at the Friday "exercises" and say, with Daniel Webster, "Mr. President, I shall enter on no encomium upon Massachusetts. She needs none. There she is. . . ." For heroism and sheer excitement, what can top Longfellow's "Listen my children and you shall hear/Of the midnight ride of Paul Revere," read to the whole family at the end of the day by father, seated in his accustomed place under the best light, in the most comfortable chair?

If we laugh at the recollection of a shock-headed boy, making his manners, then standing stiffly, feet together, as he announces: "Casablanca by Mrs. Hemans. The boy stood on the burning deck whence all but he had fled. . . ." perhaps our amusement in these uneasy times is not untinged with envy of a society secure in its sense of its own values. It was generally agreed that the United States, the land of the free and the home of the brave, was under the special protection of Providence, and that the practice of such private virtues as honesty, temperance, hard work, strict economy, and eternal hope would be rewarded not only in Heaven but right here, maybe next week.

For too long now the many-sided Victorians have had a bad press. They deserve from us now, at the minimum, an increased awareness of their versatile response to life, admiration for their solid accomplishments, charity for their follies and such paradoxes as these: The Victorians were conventionally pious, yet exhibited a pathological concern over death, which sits oddly with a professed certainty of a happier hereafter.

They supported an exacting sexual code, yet a bishop declared that there were more prostitutes than Methodists in New York City.

They fought for idealistic reforms, yet tolerated the lowest ethical standards in political and commercial life which this country has ever seen.

They congratulated themselves upon the refinement of their taste, yet found jokes about corpses, drunkenness, love affairs, immigrants, and minority groups screamingly funny.

Their popular literature was euphemistic, genteel, and bland. Yet the Victorians read advertisements in their magazines and newspapers which strike one as squalid and revolting even in our time when almost anything goes.

The Victorians were, in sum, a vigorous, innovative, creative, subjective, and self-satisfied people. It was their destiny to live in a stable social environment, with sensibilities, syndromes, and blind spots quite different from ours; and they do make interesting ancestors. We are, after all, their heirs.

Pre-Columbian goddess of childbirth.
Courtesy of Dumbarton Oaks, Washington

PREHISTORIC DISEASE AND PRIMITIVE MEDICINE

by Thomas W. and
Sharon McKern

*D*isease and injury—words so ominous to us even now that we turn from them. How much more frightening they must have been at the dawn of human existence when the slightest disability raised the ugly specter of death!

Man has no dread like that of ill health. Pain and anxiety take their toll, and healthy individuals are prey to the illnesses of their relatives. Yet in reconstructing the history of mankind, few other phenomena mirror so faithfully the environment and behavior of man.

There exists in any era an intricate relationship between man's lifeways and the afflictions he endures, for ecology and culture dictate the terms on which human mishaps may occur. The first unrecorded death by stone hand ax hundreds of thousands of years ago is as true to its time as the first known space fatality less than two years ago.

Specific human diseases and injuries are inextricably bound with the facts of man's existence, whenever and wherever he lives. It is this relationship—traced through ancient skeletal remains, mummified tissues, fragmentary records, and, sometimes, even works of art —that enables us to reconstruct the total life of early man.

Past evidences of morbidity, susceptibilities and immunities characteristic of previous human populations, help to trace historical relationships and yield implications for the present diagnosis of disease in terms of incidence and etiology. And past evidence of successes (and failures) in combating the effects of debilitation help to explain the rise not only of cults and religions but of whole societies as well.

The "healthy savage" myth perpetrated by contemporary romantics depicts ancient man as a hardy specimen who, spared the stresses of rapid-pace, 20th-century living, possessed a high resistance to bacterial infection and a natural immunity to disease. The myth, as we shall see, is built on more than whimsy, yet early man fared hardly so well as it implies. The truth is that man always has had to deal with disease and injury. Since the moment he diverged from his ancestral anthropoid stock, he had been so plagued.

It is impossible to pinpoint the time at which man first attempted to heal himself. From studies of nonhuman primates, however, we can assume that the earliest human forms treated their wounds and illnesses instinctively. They licked and sucked at the site of pain to relieve discomfort.

Such responses represent no formalization of medical procedure nor, indeed, any understanding of cause-and-effect. They are simple steps taken to alleviate pain, and they differ very little from the automatic licking undertaken by a puppy with a lacerated forepaw.

But to the primitive mind disease is mysterious and

invisible, and it strikes without predictability. It must somehow be handled, and so early man evolved a ritualistic behavior based on sympathetic magic—the treatment, for example, of jaundice with juices extracted from the leaves of yellow plants. He devised specific forms of supernatural address in order to gain relief from his otherwise untreatable agonies.

Gradually there grew a system of medical specialization with medicine men, sorcerers, and shamans prescribing treatment through mystic incantation and exorcism. A very large part of healing is magical, for if the affliction is believed to be caused by magic, how else must the cure be effected?

However primitive, disease magic represents the first formalized attempt to deal with such miseries as fever, laceration, and broken bone. And magical procedure is surprisingly effective. It frequently prescribes measures possessing sound therapeutic properties—poultices, herb potions, sweat baths, massages, and purgatives. The Indians of pre-Columbian America, for example, were particularly impressed with the healing powers of the common enema.

Modern pharmacology has borrowed more than a few drugs from the vast stockpile of substances extracted by primitives from seeds, barks, herbs, roots, leaves, minerals, and insects. Other treatments were, in themselves, useless. But the mere presence of a specialist—be he sorcerer or physician—by the sickbed is potent medicine.

As man progressed culturally from a purely biological existence, he was confronted by (and invented) dramatic new wounds with which to deal. When first he began to fashion weapons from sticks and stones for use in satisfying his carniverous appetite, it was inevitable that he himself might one day become a target. Deep cuts and wounds inflicted by crude stone weapons exposed subsurface bodily structures, and man began to learn something of his own anatomy. This knowledge was quickly expanded through the butchering of animals for food.

We know that prehistoric man of the Upper Paleolithic, some 35,000 years ago, was at least vaguely familiar with visceral topography. His cave walls are covered with vivid paintings of hearts pierced by stone spears, often with trails of flowing blood.

In treating disease or injury, the first measure taken by man, either primitive or advanced, is to find the cause. When a wound results from a foreign object in the body, removal is the only possible procedure.

Early man may have imagined a magical impetus behind the deadly spear, but he hardly expected magic to bear the burden of repair alone. And crude surgery began to flower. With some basic knowledge of anatomy, there was no need to resort to the slow and often ineffectual sucking out of splinters and other foreign bodies. These now could be cut out, or probed with fine, hand-fashioned blades.

Blood-letting—and with it, the release of evil spirits —was an innovation of this time. And it is possible that some wounds were surgically repaired—lip cuts among early American Indians were occasionally sewn closed with strands of human hair.

Not all wounds were those of aggression. Clumsy feet and faulty judgment led to accidental bone fractures, and these are common in the fossil record not only for man but for his primate relatives.

Splinting was an early treatment. The placing of moist, soothing clay or mud on an injured limb is almost instinctive. Either substance forms a natural cast as it dries and serves to immobilize the injured part, subsequently to ease pain and promote healing. Intentional immobilization quickly followed, and the addition of sticks, bound into place with any pliable material at hand, occurred as a predictable improvement.

Simple limb fractures are seldom fatal, though they may be excruciatingly painful. This was quite a lucky thing for ancient man, for reduction of fractures in the absence of anesthetic is an awesome task, apparently beyond the skill or patience of early practitioners. The site of healed breaks in early skeletal material is characterized by extensive callus formation and shortening.

Cranial fractures, not surprisingly, constitute a much more serious business, and scalp infections must have been severe. The high recovery rate presumed on the basis of recovered skeletal remains argues for either the application of antiseptic dressings (unlikely, in the light of the lice-laden hair of most mummies) or for that persistent notion of high bacterial resistance among primitive peoples.

But numerous groups dared to tamper with the skull. One of the most extraordinary of the early medical practices is that of trephination, or trepanning—the surgical removal of portions of the skull vault. Examples are known from Peru, Mexico, France, and Canada. One of the earliest comes from Stuttgart, in a site dating from about 3,000 B.C.—an amazingly early time for man to dabble in cranial surgery.

Some experts maintain that trephination was undertaken to cure epilepsy and other "madness" diseases. Others talk in terms of curing severe headache. In Peru, the operation apparently was performed to alleviate pain of depressed skull fractures caused by the vicious star-shaped maces hurled by slingshots in that time and region.

It is possible, too, that the surgery was performed with ritualistic intent, perhaps to secure discs of human skull for amulets and charms. But these could have easily been obtained from corpses without resorting to depleting the ranks of the living. We may never know for certain.

The amazing thing about trephination is that it was

successful, and the most skillful trepanners were the pre-Columbian Peruvians. It is estimated that a majority of their patients survived the ordeal. Numerous skulls evidence not one healed trephination but traces of from *one to six subsequent operations,* convincing enough proof of the surgeon's skill and the patient's faith.

It has been suggested that post-operative dressings, probably of resin or balsam, aided in recovery. This theory is based on frequent recognition in the skeletal remains of a typical bony inflammation known as osteitis, often sharply delineated on the trepanned surface. Since sections of the scalp must be removed prior to cutting, sawing, or drilling into the skull itself, it seems likely that dressings were used to hasten scalp healing.

No evidence survives for anesthesia, but man was familiar from early times with various herb drugs and it is more feasible to assume that a patient contemplating trephination would take advantage of any sleep-inducing potion available to him. Most primitive peoples boast a wide stock of animal and vegetable substances that can be turned to use as narcotics and sedatives.

Widely associated with trephination is a line of bony inflammation called "sincipital-T injury," apparently caused by the application of boiling oils or resins subsequent to scalp incisions. Cauterization and burn injuries, of course, cannot predate the use of fire, which was discovered at least as early as 500,000 years ago.

Fire itself offered to early man much in the way of preventive medicine—its use provided warmth and comfort, particularly for ailing individuals, and improved means of food preparation. Controlled use, too, kept dangerous animals at bay.

But with fire came a new type of injury—the burn. Ancient man probably treated burns with salves made of ground acacia nuts, which contain tannic acid. And fire was put to use as a new method for treating other injuries.

Examples of cauterization, like those seen in sincipital-T injuries, date from the later stone ages of Europe, Asia, Africa, and Peru. Certainly cauterization is common among contemporary non-literates who choose this means of stopping blood flow following injury or deliberate mutilation.

Also, we can safely assume that cauterization has a relatively ancient history. Human skeletal remains from Shanidar in Iraq, dating from 50,000 years ago, are believed to represent both cauterization and amputation among the Neanderthals. Aurignacian cave paintings drawn 38,000 years ago depict human hands with missing fingers—too many to suggest accidental loss.

Great antiquity would not be surprising for amputation, for punishment by this means—cutting off fingers, toes, noses, ears, and tongues—is common among primitive peoples. Amputation even of entire limbs as a form of self-castigation is known for American Indians from 1800 A.D.

Early man, who had a decidedly practical nature, must have been able also to recognize a hopeless injury when he saw one and to realize when a badly injured part would be better removed.

It is often difficult to say just where medical practice leaves off and ritualistic operations begin. In the case of early amputations, digital loss may represent accidental injuries or—and it is equally likely—deliberate ceremonial mutilation.

Dental mutilation—the extraction, filing, or inlaying of certain teeth—dates from the Upper Paleolithic in Africa and from the Neolithic in Asia Minor and Japan. The practice is common in the New World among the ancient Maya.

Here strikingly elaborate dental inlays of jade and pyrite are found in great number. The motivation for this activity obviously combines religious and cosmetic urges, yet in numerous cases—as where the upper front teeth were literally torn from their sockets—some medical treatment must have accompanied the operation.

The same must be said for ritualistic practices related to sex. Genital mutilations appear throughout the world; few peoples are entirely unacquainted with them. Circumcision, the circular abscission of the penis foreskin, is almost universal. Mummies and drawings dating from as early as 5000 B.C. attest to widespread adherence to the custom for boys and girls entering puberty. Fragmentary records survive to suggest that the surgeries were performed to honor dead heroes and to placate angry gods.

Excision, the female counterpart to circumcision, involves the surgical removal of a part or the whole of the female clitoris. It has a more restricted geographical distribution but an equal antiquity. Such operations may be performed to lessen the sensuality of tribal females, thus insuring faithfulness to their mates. But in other locales, reference is made to *increased* sexual pleasure, fuller hygiene control, and easier parturition.

Infibulation, noted among Roman children, consists of closing, by clasps or stitches, the female vulva to prevent copulation and so limit illegitimate pregnancies. And there are endless variations, some known from ancient records, others through oral tradition.

Subincision, practiced today by most Australian tribes, is a surgical technique which opens the ventral portion of the penis from the urinary meatus to the scrotum. This act represents the most extraordinary of all sexual mutilations. Horror at the thought of such surgery is hardly confined to the western world—many young men flee their tribes rather than submit to the operation.

The purpose of the sexual surgeries appears to be

largely therapeutic, designed to prevent disease and injury and—where magic is prevalent—to keep at bay certain supernatural mishaps. Often, the surgery is performed as an act of human sacrifice, that of a part of the organ to insure success of the whole, and so promote the fertility so necessary for the survival of the group.

Treatment in prehistory included prolonged rest, coupled with heat and smoke from a urine-dampened fire. Infections and death were common results, yet the customs continue today among numerous peoples, often with surgical tools no more sophisticated than the crude stone knife used thousands of years ago. It was the beneficial effects of circumcision noted among the Jews, who followed the tradition as a sacred covenant between them and their Lord, which led to its adoption throughout the western world as a hygienic measure.

For numerous afflictions there was no cure, no hope in those early days of abatement. Of these, we have only skeletal remains to indicate disease patterns and incidences. They tell little of the fear and despair which must have accompanied their occurrence, or of the frenzied efforts by puzzled ancients to strike back against invisible enemies. But they hint at the human condition before recorded history.

With the exception of fractures, arthritis appears to be the oldest and most common of all bone pathologies. It stalked the caves before man, striking at the dinosaur and the cave bear. Arthritis is universal in time and in space: No humans—regardless of climate, diet, or life habits—have escaped its rigors. It crippled the Neanderthals, leaving them with stooped backs and gnarled hands; it lodged also in their jaws, a painful tribute to the coarse and gritty diet they favored.

Arthritis accompanied man through his history, striking wherever food supplies were minimal and life-stress severe, and complicated wounds by inducing new

55

bony growth or fusing injured bone elements.

Tumors, benign and malignant, have tormented man from his distant beginnings. Simple and harmless new growths, generally reactions to injury, are common in the fossil record. One is seen in the thighbone of *Pithecanthropus erectus,* who lived some half a million years ago in Java.

Malignant growths are not nearly so common, and it is here that we see the most obvious pathological differences between modern and ancient populations. While modern peoples suffer millions of deaths yearly from stomach, bowel, breast, and lung cancers, carcinoma in early times is rare.

Some authorities, convinced that cancer is emotionally triggered, blame the stress of modern living for its higher incidence today. More likely, since carcinoma kills the elderly, its scarcity in the fossil record serves only to point up a shorter life-span for early peoples.

It is with urbanization that man began to encounter bacterial infections. With the rise of agriculture, the varied diets of the stone age were replaced by staple grain crops, and for many people the old, isolated life was traded for sedentary occupations. Now the natural factors which confined infections to far-flung nomadic bands and controlled population numbers were gone; man began to live in unsanitary and overcrowded conditions. Travel and urbanization favored epidemic diseases and endemic infections.

Sinusitis appears early in pre-Columbian Peru and in Egypt, where it originated in the irritation of nasal linings caused by the dust-laden air of that region. When chronic and severe, it led to acute mastoiditis, an affliction rare in earlier times but seen as early as 45,000 years ago in the skull of Rhodesian man, whose problems were complicated by a set of badly rotting teeth.

Tuberculosis began to take its toll. It is common in Europe from Neolithic times, and appears earlier in

Egypt, where men contracted it by drinking milk from infected cattle.

Syphilis appeared and spread with devastating results. Authorities disagree as to origin. Some believe it to be a New World disease, but the presence of syphilitic lesions in skeletal material from ancient times in the Old World suggests that it was introduced into the western hemisphere by Spanish conquistadores, where it decimated New World populations, rendering them helpless before their European invaders. Both Australia and South Africa were free of both syphilis and tuberculosis until white infiltration carried them in.

No disease in the history of mankind aroused so much dread and horror as leprosy. It affects only the human species and is spread by direct man-to-man infection, it is a disease inherent to times of travel and social intercourse, and it strikes wherever there exists dirt and poverty. Treatment from as early as 600 B.C. included such desperate measures as oil purges, snake bites, and scorpion stings.

The Egyptian historian Manetho in the second century before Christ writes that the Israelites were driven from Egypt because they were leprous. The Bible (Leviticus 13) prescribes harsh and stringent requirements under Mosaic Law in regard to the handling of lepers.

Leprosy is not seen in New World skeletal remains; we must assume it was introduced in historic times by the Europeans who spread their ghastly collection of other diseases—smallpox, diphtheria, cholera, typhus, and—the most dreaded of all—plague.

Urbanization, too, has brought us the deficiency diseases—rickets, scurvy, and osteomalacia, that fearful softening of the bones that leads to death through exhaustion. These diseases come with industrial growth, when living conditions become crowded and no heed is given to the need for sunlight and ventilation.

Of all the body parts, it is the teeth that are most

durable and survive most often for analysis. From them, we know that caries, alveolar abscesses, periodontitis, and calculus deposits have tormented man throughout his existence. Pyorrhea and resulting abscesses appear from the time of the Neanderthals. Caries, however, increase in incidence with the Neolithic, when improved methods of food production revolutionized dietary habits.

In general, flesh-eaters had a better time of it than the growers of carbohydrates. But few generalizations are possible as diet, mode of food preparation, and mineral content of native waters diversify the dental problems of each population.

Congenital malformations are common from ancient times. Clubfoot has been diagnosed in the mummy of King Siptah (1225 B.C.). Poliomyelitis is suspected for another mummy dating from 3700 B.C.

We can only guess at the thousands of other afflictions endured which leave no marks on the bones or teeth, and which cannot be known from preserved mummies. We can know only that man's struggle toward the establishment of civilization was dependent upon his ability to preserve health and prolong life—and yet the very act of coming together to build communities spread new and uncontrollable diseases.

It is not until the time of the first true civilizations that we come to know how medical science began its torturous road to being. With civilization came the invention of writing, the division between prehistory and history. And with history came the dawn of true medicine.

The dawn broke in the valley of the Nile where, slowly, the Egyptians began to accumulate the trappings of civilization. It is here, from preserved mummies and ancient papyri, that we learn of man's first concentrated efforts to build a medical science.

They first built upon magic, because they retained

the heritage handed down through the earlier sorcerers. All illness and injury, according to Egyptian theory, resulted from invasion of the body by malevolent spirits. Treatment aimed not only toward curing the disease and prolonging life but also toward averting spiritual disaster and preparing for life in the next world.

Deliberate mummification of the dead began with the observation that bodies buried in the hot sands of the desert became dessicated and, usually, fully preserved. The Egyptians became master embalmers, leading us to expect their anatomical knowledge to be extensive.

Yet no separate or specific treatises on anatomy have been found, and no evidence exists to suggest that the early Egyptians studied anatomy by means of deliberate dissection. In fact, though their knowledge was sufficient to effect evisceration through an incision no larger than 100mm, it seems never to have occurred to them to examine the inner body while working on it in preparation of eventual resurrection. The Egyptians were familiar with body organs—they removed all of them, cleansed them, and packed them into jars which would accompany the mummy into its case. And yet they remained remarkably ignorant of bodily structure.

Analysis of preserved mummies, usually through radiography, has enabled us to know many of the diseases from which the Egyptians suffered and died. Arteriosclerosis is first seen in such remains, one example found in the aorta of a Pharaoh dating from 1225 B.C. Silicosis and anthracosis, triggered by the inhalation of dust and carbon, are common. Emphysema, resulting from asthma and chronic bronchitis, is known, as well as pneumonia and pleurisy. Egyptians suffered, too, with kidney and gallstones and were plagued by cirrhosis of the liver, chronic appendicitis, and bladder infections.

But it is the medical documents, inscribed upon papyrus and preserved for centuries, that tell most of these early days of medicine. Seven medical papyri so far have been discovered and translated.

Most are fragmentary or carelessly written. All are difficult to date. Those surviving represent copies of earlier texts with numerous additions, deletions, and errors. Almost all are threaded with superstition and magic. But present, too, is a persistent notion of rational treatment, based upon procedures that worked in the past.

The incomplete London medical papyrus, dating from the 12th Dynasty, contains more than 30 sections on gynecology, with pregnancy and methods of sex determination receiving specific treatment.

The Ebers papyrus dates from the 18th Dynasty, but was first composed in the 12th Dynasty, about 2000 B.C. It contains no less than 40 groups of remedies, with appropriate spells and incantations, and 47 diagnosed cases of disease.

Prescriptions are given, most of them elaborate and citing exact and careful measurements. Others are clouded by mysticism, calling for such exotic ingredients as pig's eyes and frog-warmed-in-oil. For baldness, an animal-fat ointment was applied to the head. For "immediate" cure of blindness, more drastic measures were required: a paste of honey, pig's eyes, and ocher were poured into the ear for instantaneous restoration of sight.

The Hearst and Berlin papyri, dating from the same period, duplicate the data contained in the Ebers document and, characteristically, blend magic with medicine.

But during the 18th Dynasty relatively sophisticated surgical techniques demonstrate an admirable concept of man's physical makeup, especially in view of the time—more than a thousand years before Hippocrates.

The Edwin Smith papyrus from this time is the earliest surgical treatise yet discovered and the earliest non-magical medical papyrus. It was possible by this time to reduce fractures, stop hemorrhage, extract foreign bodies, effect castration and minor amputation, drain cysts and tumors, and cleanse and suture open wounds. Salves, compresses, gargles, eardrops, and enemas were recommended, replacing the older raven's-blood and goat's-dung-in-yeast prescriptions designed to insult and thus exorcise the causative spirit.

The Smith papyrus also reflects a realistic appraisal of current medical skill. Each described ailment is accompanied by a prognosis, which may follow any of three paths from "an ailment which I will treat," to "an ailment with which I will contend," to "an ailment not to be treated." Some wounds, therefore, were beyond the physician's skill and no treatment was attempted. Treatments recommended are practical; many are sensible and remain in use today.

Medical specialization originates in Egypt. Obstetrics was performed by qualified midwives, and each physician concentrated upon a particular area of competence —the eyes, for example, or the stomach. Physicians were held in high accord and occupied high social status, indicating an awareness of the dangers of disease despite a wide belief in the happy afterlife.

With Egypt comes the beginning chapter in the story of medical advance, and the end of our present concern. "In medical knowledge," wrote Homer, "the Egyptians leave the rest of the world behind." The path toward medical competence took no direct route, but here in Egypt, where specialization was born and writing came into being to preserve what is known from the past, the journey began. We travel still.

BLACK DEATH
AND
THE MATURING
OF MAN

by Bruce C. Williams

*T*hree thousand years ago the
Philistines captured the Israelites' sacred Ark of the
Covenant on the bloody battle plain of Ebenezer and
brought the wrath of God down upon their people.
According to *I Samuel*, ". . . He smote the men of the
city both small and great, and they had *emerods* in
their secret parts" —hemorrhoids in the groin, swollen
lymph glands, *buboes*—the classic onset of bubonic
plague. Shortly, the demoralized Philistines returned the
Ark to Bethshemesh with peace offerings, golden images
of emerods and mice. These "mice" were obviously rats.
The ancients knew too well that wholesale death among
the rats meant death for them.

In the centuries that followed, plague swept westward out of Asia and into the heartland of Europe in
three pandemic waves. Nothing else in man's history

has killed his kind in such numbers or spread blind panic on so grand a scale. Nothing else has so roused the beast in him toward his fellow man. Nor has any other agent of disaster pressed him so steadily into acknowledging his ignorance, renouncing his superstitions, and conquering his fear and despair that he might find the truth.

When monarchs were monarchs in every sense and heads were expendable, court counselors rarely said, "I don't know." The pressure for explanations grew hot, and men of learning blithely, and prudently, invented science-fictional rigamaroles. Guy de Chauliac, the celebrated surgeon to the court of Pope Clement VI, granted current respectability to the ancient theory of *miasmi,* disease-bearing pollution of the atmosphere due, he said, to the conjunction of Saturn, Jupiter, and Mars in the sign of Aquarius. Variations of this theory stubbornly hung on for the next half thousand years, but another titanic storm was brewing in the East. The second pandemic would take man around another bend on the road to reason.

In 1346 hordes of plague-infected Tartars stormed the wealthy Genoese trading port of Caffa in the Crimea, and the Italian merchant residents fled home by sea. By April of 1348 the Death was rampaging from Messina to Florence, and Italy's metropolitan centers virtually ceased to exist as organized societies. As cemeteries filled, the corpses were dumped into trenches, sometimes covered, sometimes not.

One remnant of order, the *Monatti,* was feared as much as plague itself. This was a corps of plague attendants, mostly liberated galley slaves with bells on their legs as a badge of authority. The wretched folk of Italy's stricken cities cringed to see those jingling monsters dragging the dead, and not quite dead, to the pits. Those who could, fled, like Boccaccio's imaginary dandies and ladies who sealed themselves off in a Florentine country house. The ribald stories they told to pass the time make up the *Decameron* in which Boccaccio resurrects his already dead love, Maria d'Aquino, in the person of Fiametta.

The pestilence spread and with it the rumor that Jews were fouling the wells with plague poison. The senseless brutality which followed would not be equalled until the genocide campaigns of the Third Reich. The madness reached a pinnacle in Basle where the entire Jewish population was herded into a wooden building on an island in the Rhine and burned to death.

While Europeans from Spain to Germany boarded over their wells and hounded the Jews, Edward III crushed the French at Crecy and Calais. His armies returned to England with plundered silks and jewelry—and plague. He staged victory tournaments throughout the countryside and founded the Order of the Garter, but the epidemic which followed killed half the population of England and Wales.

Across the channel, the plague epidemic of 1348-49 revived one of the queerest mixtures of piety, masochism, and sadism ever known, the Flagellants. They wandered over the Continent preaching that salvation for the soul and protection from plague lay solely in abuse of the body and flogging each other till the blood flowed.

It ended when Pope Clement VI, recognizing its threat to the sovereignty of the priesthood, ordered his inquisitors to suppress the movement with burnings at the stake. In 1532 the church tackled plague in a higher arena. Irregular appearances in the heavens were routinely associated with recurring plague so, when a comet blazed into the sky, Pope Clement VII simply excommunicated the intruder.

England's Good Queen Bess displayed more common sense when plague again struck London in 1563. She hied herself to Windsor Castle and ordered a gallows erected in the courtyard—this for anyone, high or low, who came from London a-calling. The preacher of St. Paul's Cross intoned, "The cause of plagues, is sinne, if you looke to it well, and the cause of sinne are plays, therefore the cause of plagues are playes."

More sinister accusations had been leveled a year earlier in Milan where another epidemic was raging. Here, the hysterical cry of *pestis manufacta,* plague salving, reached a crescendo. Normally friendly folk spied their neighbors smearing Satan's evil ointment on the houses of their neighbors. Two, so accused, Commissioner William Platea and John Jacob Mora, the barber, protested their innocence. Stretched on the rack, however, with arms and legs slowly wrenched from the sockets, the two confessed.

They were then driven through the town in a cart, and before each house where salving had been reported their flesh was crimped with glowing tongs. Before Mora's house, each had his right hand chopped off. Finally, at the prescribed execution site, the wretched pair were spread-eagled on the wheel and their bones methodically smashed with iron bars.

From nation to nation, fear of plague was the same. Only the reaction of people differed and, to The Great Dying, we owe one of the most artful religious pageants of all time. In 1633 the disease killed eighty-four citizens of the tiny Bavarian mountain village of Oberammergau. Stunned, the men and women of the town gathered in fear and love and looked to their God. They made the vow they still keep three centuries later, to re-enact the Passion and death of Christ every tenth year.

Others sought less lofty air for the achievement of less lofty goals during the Marseilles epidemic of 1628. There, *Vinaigre des Quatre Voleurs,* Vinegar of the Four Thieves, supposedly protected its users from infection while plundering the homes of the dead. *Vinaigre des Quatre Voleurs* won't be found on any cosmetic counters today, but another plague water, Eau de Cologne, concocted by the Italian Giovanni Maria Farina in 1700, has made a place for itself around the civilized world.

Plague prevention, on a personal level, followed quite a different vogue in London where the citizenry seized upon the medicinal properties of tobacco, recently introduced from the Colonies. Samuel Pepys' diary records that, on being alarmed by the sight of plague quarantine crosses on the houses, he "was forced to buy some roll tobacco to smell and chaw, which took away the apprehension." Eaton schoolboys were required to smoke every morning during plague epidemics and the historian, Thomas Hearne, wrote that one Tom Rogers was "never whipped so much in his life as he was one morning for not smoaking."

Plague prevention also occupied the thoughts of London's civil authorities where the disease continued to flare despite the attention previously paid to wrathful gods, designing demons, and wicked mortals. By 1592, though the concept had assumed only the haziest shape, plague was officially regarded as infectious. The clergy had offered an embarrassing obstacle, so that General Plague Orders issued in that year by the London Privy Council forbade preaching the doctrine that plague was a punishment for sin.

But the outbreaks continued in 1603, 1625, 1636 and culminated in 1665 with a staggering blow, wiping out sixty-eight thousand lives in a total population of less than half a million. The epidemic continued at a slower pace into 1666 and many contend that Londoners owe a debt of gratitude to a little bakery in Pudding Lane hard by London Bridge. The shop caught fire in the early hours of Sunday, September 2, and the Great London Fire which followed destroyed four fifths of the walled city and millions of rats and their breeding places. Coincidence, perhaps, but London hasn't experienced a major outbreak of plague since.

Nine years after the London plagues subsided, the first major advance in the understanding of the disease was scored by a man who went to his grave not knowing what he'd done. Anthony van Leeuwenhoek was no scientist in the formal sense. He seems to have been, at various times, an usher, an upholsterer, a clerk, a modest citizen of the little pottery-making town of Delft on the River Schie in the south of Holland. He was fascinated by the idea that there were beings, too small to see, yet alive and purposefully moving.

He made lenses of extremely short focal length and opened up the world of the microbe. He saw blood corpuscles, sperm cells, yeast cells, and—bacteria. In a series of letters to the Royal Society of London beginning in 1674, van Leeuwenhoek described what he'd seen. To him and to the society, these were intriguing academic curiosities—nothing more. Yet the existence of microbes had been established. Men of science would continue to ponder the significance of that fact.

Van Leeuwenhoek's reports were gathering dust on the shelves of the Royal Society when, in 1720, the trading vessel, *Grand Saint-Antoine,* under the command of a Captain Chataud, put into the port of Marseilles bringing passengers and a cargo of cotton, silk, and muslin from the East. One passenger, six crewmen, and the ship's surgeon had died en route and were buried at sea. The port surgeon who dutifully recorded this event as due to *malignant pestilential fever* assigned the passengers to the routine fourteen day quarantine, the crew to the *lazzaretta,* a loosely supervised quarantine clinic for seamen.

From this nearly ideal operations center, the crew immediately busied themselves with the age-old sideline of the merchant seaman. Silks were probably the favorite items of cargo pilfered from the hold and smuggled ashore to the highest bidders. In the course of discharging legitimate cargo into the quarantine sheds, several wharf hands and crewmen, a cabin boy, and a quarantine guard fell ill with fever. This time the port surgeon cited "bad food." He himself died a few days later, and several inhabitants of the city's interior developed fever and the dreaded buboes.

Too late the city's authorities recalled recent reports of plague epidemics in Palestine and Syria. Captain Chataud was pointlessly imprisoned in the infamous Chateau d'If, his quarantined cargo was burned, and the *Grand Saint-Antoine* was towed to the Isle de Jarre and set afire. But the smuggled goods, and plague, had already found their way throughout Marseilles and into the suburbs. By the end of August, 1721, thirty-nine thousand of the city's total population of ninety thousand were dead. Before the pestilence had run its course through the environs of Marseilles, eighty-eight thousand lives had been wiped out.

Rather than settling the conflict between the champions of miasma and those who preached contagion, the Marseilles disaster merely stiffened the resolve of both. The girls in Marseilles' many convents escaped completely though surrounded by plague. To contagionists, this was proof enough that isolation meant protection. Proponents of miasma retorted that the girls' survival was simply a manifestation of the power of their faith. But, at least, medical opinion had advanced to squabbling over one natural cause as against another. Belief in the influence of the divine, the diabolical, and the evil doings of men was fading.

With the subsiding of the Marseilles epidemic, the rampaging phase of the second pandemic came to an end. In its first three violent years it had slaughtered twenty million Europeans, one quarter of the population. For nearly four more centuries plague ranged across the Continent killing additional millions whose numbers will never be known with certainty. In the relative quiet that followed, the search for the causes of the disease lost some of its frenzy and was advanced another giant stride. As it had been with van Leeuwenhoek, the deed was brought off by a layman with no designs against plague.

It is one of those curious oversights of history that the name of Agostino Bassi of Lodi, Italy, is missing from virtually all of our standard references. Yet it was he who, at the cost of his sight, proved that van Leeuwenhoek's microbes were the root cause of disease. With already failing eyes, Bassi worked over his microscopes for twenty years tracing the cause and effect pattern of muscardine, the silkworm disease which was destroying the European silk industry.

Though largely forgotten by the public, Bassi is commemorated in the terminology and annals of medicine. The parasitic fungus which greeted Bassi's weakening eyes as he opened the door on microbial infection still bears his name: *Botrytis Bassiana*. The *Bulletin of History of Medicine of the Johns Hopkins Institute of Medicine* salutes him thus, ". . . pathogenic bacteriology . . . was founded by Bassi and not by Pasteur, Koch, or others. As a consequence, Pasteur and Koch and the others are only followers, however glorious and pre-eminent, of Bassi."

As the third and last pandemic plague of history began, the teachings of Pasteur, the Frenchman, and Koch, the German, were destined to play a key role, in duet. Plague appeared quietly in the small treaty port of Pakhoi on the southern coast of China in 1867. It came and went for the next twenty-seven years in China's trading ports, then flared into a major epidemic in March, 1894, killing forty thousand in Canton. Two months later the disease appeared in Hong Kong. Here,

The French classicist Nicholas Poussin painted the Plague of Ashdod, *the first of his narrative scenes from the Old Testament.*

the death rate was lower, but the vested interest of foreigners was higher and brought about one of the closest races in medical history.

The Japanese physician, Professor Shibasaburo Kitasato, student of Robert Koch, arrived in Hong Kong on the twelfth of June. He was followed three days later by the Swiss bacteriologist, Alexandre Emile Yersin, recently of the Pasteur Institute in Paris. Within days of each other, possibly within hours, both men found the villain under their microscopes in blood and tissue specimens taken from plague victims. We know it today as *Pasteurella Pestis.*

It matters little which man actually first brought P. Pestis into focus, for the omnipotent hodgepodge of miasma, witchcraft, human evil, and divine wrath was finally on its way to the scrap heap. Yet millions more would die as the pestilence again spread westward and science struggled with the last major riddle, the mode of transmission of P. Pestis from the ill to the healthy.

The generally accepted Alimentary Theory held that the bacilli were discharged in infected human and animal excrement, picked up on the body surfaces of rats, mice, flies, and cockroaches and transfered to human foodstuffs to complete the cycle of infection. One dissenter was D. P. L. Simond, a researcher in Bombay where plague was raging out of control. Many, including Simond, no longer regarded the rats as man's hapless fellow victims but, rather, as the prime mover in the migration of P. Pestis. But how?

Simond proved that P. Pestis died rapidly when removed from its warm-blooded host and could rarely be recovered alive from stored grain or cloth. Further, exposing laboratory rats to heavily contaminated material failed to result in plague to any significant degree, yet merely pricking the skin with a needle bearing the bacilli routinely resulted in disease. P. Pestis, he reasoned, must invade the body through a skin puncture. But, again, how?

Simond re-examined the evidence of the centuries. Throughout the body's vast lymphatic network, lymph glands stand at the ready to trap bacteria. Those guarding the leg route are situated in the groin; those for the arms, in the armpits; those for the head, in the neck. As millions of plague bacilli are stopped on their way toward the body's interior, these glands become engorged, forming the familiar and dreaded bubo. Also, small pustules sometimes appeared on the feet of the afflicted, not, however, on the highly exposed sole but on the thinner skin of the ankle.

What, then, could carry P. Pestis from rat to rat, from rat to man, from man to man? What could function as a natural innoculating needle? What would prefer to do its lethal work on the thin-skinned ankles of men and on the similarly vulnerable heads of rats? What could reasonably be expected to desert a cooling carcass and seek out a new and warmer host? To Simond, the answer had to be the flea and, though he lacked the apparatus to prove his theory, others would shortly do it for him. Centuries of superstitious dread, misdirected brutality, stubborn misconception, and errant guesswork were drawing to a close.

One nagging question remained unanswered: Man had obviously lived with fleas since, and probably long before, he got up off his knuckles and walked erect. Yet most of that time he was free of plague. In 1914, at the Lister Institute in London, A. W. Bacot and C. J. Martin saw the answer unfold under their dissecting microscopes. Plague was not only a disease of rats and men but also of fleas, or some fleas. They, too, were ill.

Of the sixty-odd strains known to exist, one was particularly vulnerable. *Xenopsylla Cheopis* owes its infamous fame to its peculiar digestive apparatus. The stomach of X. Cheopis quickly becomes "blocked" with multiplying plague bacilli and the valve which normally acts to allow its meal of blood to flow inward but not outward, stops functioning. X. Cheopis' further attempts to satisfy its hunger result in its vomiting the germ-laden mess back into its host. Its cousins, happily feeding on our dogs and cats, suffer no such indigestion.

With its mysteries solved, plague has been largely eliminated by preventive measures. When prevention fails, antibiotics now effect a ninety-five percent recovery rate. But plague is still with us and probably will be for all time in the *sylvatic* form—a reservoir of infected field and forest rodents around the world.

The only foreseeable catastrophe with the potential of so disrupting the orderly processes of our society as to turn this killer loose again is widespread nuclear warfare. Whether men will ever cringe to hear again the dread call echoing in their streets, "Bring out your dead," rests now with the captains of our ships of state.

JUVENILE DELINQUENCY, THEN AND NOW

by Albert G. Hess

Juvenile misconduct—which comprises grave crime as well as pranks and trifles—is by no means a characteristic feature peculiar to our country and our age. It existed at all times. As revealed in historical documents, most nations knew it well, regardless of race, religion, or form of government:

"Where have you been?"

"Nowhere."

"If you didn't go anywhere, why must you be loitering? Go to school, . . . recite your assignment . . . When you have finished and reported to the teacher, come to me and don't just walk the streets. Did I make myself clear?"

This is not a modern worried father speaking to his truant and trouble-prone son. These words were uttered approximately three thousand years ago, according to a Sumerian tablet in the museum of the University of Pennsylvania. Professor Samuel Noah Kramer calls its contents "the first case of juvenile delinquency."

In Deuteronomy, in the Old Testament, Chapter 21, 18-21, we read about the "stubborn and rebellious son, which will not obey the voice of his father, or the voice of his mother, and that, when they have chastened him, will not hearken unto them," a son who is "a glutton and a drunkard." All the men of the city shall "stone him with stones, that he die."

While juvenile misbehavior appears to be a perennial problem, society's ways of dealing with it, and—especially—its tolerance toward it, have been undergoing significant changes. To illustrate this, let us look at the case histories of Charles Cunningham and Anna Richards.

The evening of May 16, 1805, two teenage boys were gambling in the kitchen of Eichelberger's tavern in York, Pennsylvania. The youngsters were engaged in hustlecap, a game played by shaking and tossing coins in a cap. One of the boys was eighteen-year-old Charles Cunningham who had been "bound" from the poorhouse to innkeeper Eichelberger six years before.

After a while, Charles and his young friend, Joseph Rothrock, took off for another tavern. There they continued gambling until Charles won all his friend's money, plus a silver brooch, a box, and a handkerchief. As they played hustlecap, the boys drank whiskey and "cideroyal."

"I was in liquor, though as well as in my senses as I am now," Charles recalled in *The Dying Confessions of Charles Cunningham.*

Later they switched from hustlecap to dice. Luck changed hands; Joseph started to win. When the innkeeper's son, John Heckendorn, insisted on counting the game, Charles became uneasy. He was suspicious that the two might be conniving to cheat him. Quarrel ensued. In a fit of drunken rage, he led Joseph into a dark alley, with the intent to kill the latter with a knife. But the knife fell out of his hand. Instead, Charles stated himself, "[I] sprung upon him, and grasped him by the neck with both my hands, placing both my thumbs in his throat, and squeezing with all might until he fell down and appeared to be dead."

When Joseph appeared to regain consciousness, Charles, taking a small piece of twine from his pocket, tied it around Joseph's neck, and proceeded to choke him to death. Then he lifted up the body face down and dashed it on the ground four or five times. "I then committed a most horrid indignity on the dead body, for which I cannot otherwise account, than that it was done by the immediate instigation of the Devil."

A few months later, on September 19, 1805, Charles was executed.

On March 6, 1857, Caroline Cowles Richards, who lived with her grandfather, a prominent banker, in Canandaigua, New York, wrote in her diary about her younger sister:

"Anna and her set will have to square accounts with Mr. Richards tomorrow, for nine of them ran away from school this afternoon . . . They went out to Mr. Saccett's where they were making maple sugar. Mr. and Mrs. Saccett asked them in and gave them all the sugar they wanted, and Anna said pickles too, and bread and butter, and the more pickles they ate the more sugar they could eat. I guess they will think of pickles when Mr. Richards asks them where they were. I think Ellie Dagett and Charlie Paddock went, too, and some of the Academy boys."

Punishment followed promptly. The next day "they all had to stay after school . . . for an hour and copy Dictionary."

In their day, the case of Charles Cunningham and

that of Anna Richards would have been weighed very differently on the scales of justice than they would be today. No one in those days would have considered equating one with the other. On the one hand, there was a homicide, the result of a drunken rage, committed by one who was practically an adult and who, having come from the poorhouse, lacked social status. On the other hand, there was a minor truancy, playing hooky and indulging in maple syrup and pickles, carried out by nice little girls and "academy boys" from respectable families.

Yet nowadays "offenses" of such unequal weight are frequently adjudicated simply as juvenile delinquency, without naming the particular crime, in almost all the states. Indeed, the definition of juvenile delinquency can cover everything from the most trivial naughty behavior to brutal murder. And today in our most highly populated state, California, Charles Cunningham—in fact any young person up to age twenty-one—might be adjudicated as a juvenile delinquent. As this situation shows, radical changes have taken place in how we deal with juvenile delinquency today.

Just before the turn of the century, offenses by youngsters began to be shifted from adult criminal courts to juvenile courts. There, supposedly, a paternalistic and benevolent judge decided in a nonpunitive way what should be done with the young offender to make him a good citizen. While the juvenile court had —and still has—its great merits, its role as a non-criminal, benevolent agency has not always been satisfactorily fulfilled for a number of reasons, among them the lack of adequate budget and facilities that would have provided for appropriate treatment for youngsters with personality disorders.

Until the first juvenile court was established in Chicago in 1899, youngsters who committed criminal acts were, with certain exceptions, dealt with in regular

Contributing to the delinquency of a minor in the 1760's. A madam offers a young girl to a customer.

adult criminal courts. But, it must be noted, they were sent to criminal courts *only* if they were charged with committing acts for which an adult could also be punished, that is, for committing criminal acts. Other kinds of misbehavior simply never were brought into court.

With the advent of the juvenile court, a much broader definition of delinquency began to be applied. No longer need a youngster commit a criminal act to be sent to court. He could be sent under such vague charges as "being incorrigible," or for "smoking tobacco," "using intoxicating liquor," or "truancy." All these charges were applicable only to youngsters.

Moreover, neglected and dependent children—children who had committed no offenses whatsoever—also found themselves being brought before this so-called benevolent court, and often no differentiation in treatment was made between these hapless youngsters and the delinquents.

As the juvenile court idea spread from Chicago to other parts of the country in the early twentieth century, the public began to feel perfectly justified in sending youngsters to court. They also began branding more and more juvenile misbehavior as delinquency.

Earlier, authorities were reluctant to bring a child to criminal court and expose him to incarceration in the company of hardened criminals, brutal corporal punishment, and possibly even capital punishment. Generally, children were presumed unable to discern right from wrong and, therefore, were not criminally responsible. Discernment of right and wrong was never expected from an "infant," usually up to age seven. Youngsters between seven and the age of adulthood, usually fourteen, were also presumed not to possess such power of discernment, but the ability to distinguish right from wrong could be proven, and if it was determined that he could tell right from wrong, he was subject to the same harsh penalties meted out to adults. Capital punishment, however, was perhaps not carried out against children quite as frequently as some historians would have us believe.

Once the juvenile courts began handling children's cases, the public became less hesitant to send youngsters to these courts. The public's attitude was strengthened by the soothing thought that the court acted in the child's so-called "best interests." The result was the juvenile courts became overburdened with many cases which had little connection to serious delinquent behavior, such as the case that was described by New York Judge Justine Polier around 1960: "A thirteen-year-old boy was brought in as a delinquent child by a substitute teacher. He had persisted in clowning; when she tried 'to stop him' he struck out at her. The teacher knew of no previous problem with the child."

Nowadays, teachers, the police, neighbors, and parents often turn to the juvenile court to handle difficult youngsters—an "easy out" which did not exist in former times. Only recently have we come to recognize that this approach is not always beneficial to the children involved. In most cases, they do not receive appropriate help from the courts because treatment facilities are lacking. Even worse, youngsters are marked for life with a record, even though theoretically juvenile delinquents are not "criminals." Ironically, youngsters who are officially declared as delinquents often begin to think of themselves as such and to conduct themselves accordingly. Rather than deterring him from future misdeeds, the brand of delinquency often raises a youngster's status among his peers and spurs more illegal acts.

Meanwhile, the public became less and less tolerant about juvenile misbehavior in general. Much of the juvenile misbehavior that had been accepted previously as pranks or *peccadillos* started to meet with strong community disapproval and increased prosecution ef-

No distinction was made for juvenile prisoners,
guarded by policemen, waiting to appear
in a London court of 1870.

forts. For example, around 1872, when the social reformer Charles Loring Brace wrote *The Dangerous Classes of New York and Twenty Years' Work Among Them,* the police paid scant attention to the "petty plunderings" of the city's wayward boys. Yet these petty thefts by the "street rats" and "street Arabs," as they were called, were numerous.

Another example of the greater tolerance of juvenile misbehavior in the past comes from *The National Police Gazette* in the 1880's. That publication showed a picture of Vassar girls picnicking on private grounds under a "trespassers beware" sign. They had tied the protesting landlord to a tree and were tantalizing him by holding a drink under his nose, outside his reach. The caption read: "A case of slow torture. How some Vassar girls taught a crusty old land owner a lesson in good humor."

We may well wonder what would be today's reaction to such behavior. Would we tolerate it? In particular, would we tolerate it if the "offenders" were not well-bred college girls but tough youngsters from the urban ghetto?

Youth gang activities as well as juvenile delinquency have existed in the past. In 1575, in Nuremberg, Germany, a gang of thieves, aged seven to eleven, led by an older man, Hans Pack, was condemned to death. Hans was hanged before the eyes of his young accomplices who were led to believe that they, too, would be executed. However, they were reprieved, pilloried, whipped, and banished. "Although the five little rascals were very cheeky in prison, stating even in the pillory that if they had cards they would play to see who of them should be strung up first, yet when they were carried out they cried bitterly and turned around frequently to look at their companions and brothers."

In 1712 Jonathan Swift described London's upper-class "Mohocks": "One of their favorite amusements, called 'tipping the lion,' was to squeeze the nose of their victim flat upon his face and to bore out his eyes with their fingers. Among . . . [the Mohocks] were the 'sweaters,' who formed a circle round their prisoner and pricked him with their swords till he sank exhausted to the ground, the 'dancing masters,' so-called from their skill in making men caper by thrusting swords into their legs, the 'tumblers' whose favorite amusement was to set women on their head and commit various indecencies and barbarities on the limbs that were exposed. Maid-servants as they opened their masters' doors were waylaid, beaten, and their faces cut. Matrons inclosed in barrels were rolled down the steep and stony incline of Stony Hill. Watchmen were unmercifully beaten and their noses slit. Country gentlemen went to the theatre as if in time of war, accompanied by their armed retainers. A bishop's son was said to be one of the gang, and a baronet was among those who were arrested."

We can gain some notion of gang activities in nineteenth century America from the case of Charles Cunningham. To be sure, the murder he committed was a one-man crime. But Charles had belonged at the age of fifteen to a group of boys that vandalized his hometown. While being "bound" to the innkeeper, Charles had "everything plentiful" and very little work to do. He and the other boys roamed the streets at night, overthrowing carriages and water vessels. In a ropewalk they destroyed large quantities of unfinished rope and threw it into a creek. They also stole "outlines and the fish that were on the hooks."

Similarly, Anna Richards and her friends had committed the delinquency of truancy as a group or "gang," and the same may be said of the Vassar girls who tied up the property owner.

In fact, nineteenth century America—with its vast influx of immigrants, its rapidly growing industri-

Juveniles gambling in the street, 1898

alization and urbanization, its savagely demeaning slums, its exploitation of child labor—understandably became the very breeding ground of gang activity, especially in the larger cities, such as New York.

Delinquency and juvenile gangs are hardly confined to any one ethnic group. Almost all the large immigrant groups who inhabited the slums in the nineteenth century—the Irish, the Italians, the Germans, and the East European Jews—contributed to delinquency and gang activity. Often the same slum was inhabited successively by these different groups. Today we can see that the crucial precipitating factor is the slum setting rather than any particular ethnic characteristics.

In New York City, the oldest known locale of gang activity was the "Five Points" district, which is now the intersection of Worth, Baxter, and Park streets and which was then an intersection of five streets. Until 1820 the area was a relatively respectable residential area and amusement district. When the homes started to sink into the marshland on which the district originally had been founded, middle class families abandoned the area. Soon "grocery stores" of dubious nature began springing up, stores which harbored back rooms where cheap, illegal whiskey was dispensed and gang members could hang out. By 1840, the "Five Points" area had become one of the city's most despicable slums, the home of a few freed Negro slaves and a big population of new Irish immigrants, the "black sheep" of their day.

One of the district's worst gangs was the "Plug Uglies." According to Asbury, the historian of New York gangs, the term came from the big "Plug-hats"—also called "chimney-pot-hats" or "top hats"—that the gang members converted into battle helmets. They accomplished this by stuffing the hats with wool and leather and drawing them over their ears. The uniform of the "Plug Uglies" was completed by heavy boots with hob-

The return of the prodigal son, from a painting by Bida

nails for stamping on prostrate victims.

While we do not know the exact ages of the gang members, we can deduce they must have been quite young. Brace writes of them as "youthful ruffians," and calls them *"enfants perdus* grown up to young manhood." Junior auxiliaries were a common feature of many of the Five Points gangs, such as "Forty Little Thieves"—the younger branch of the "Forty Thieves." (That group was led for a while by a girl called Wild Maggie Carson, who was later rehabilitated and taught to be a seamstress.) These junior gang members took their cues from the older ones in everything from appearance to speech to deed.

Among the most damaging of the younger gangs were the Little Day Break Boys. Like their seniors— the Day Break Boys—they operated on New York's waterfront. The Day Break Boys were only one of several river pirate gangs. There were also the Swamp Angels, the Slaughter-housers, and the Short Tails. They operated from small boats, moving around the wharves and vessels, stealing whatever they could lay their hands on.

One gang of youngsters active around the turn of the century was a group of twenty to thirty pickpockets. Their leader, Crazy Butch, was in his late teens. He used to ride slowly on a bicycle, while the members of his gang walked along on the sidewalks. Then Crazy Butch would run into a pedestrian and proceed to hurl abuse at him. This inevitably and immediately drew an angry crowd whose pockets were promptly picked by the waiting boys.

Early twentieth century writers sometimes described contemporary gangs rather indulgently. J. Adams Puffer, a principal of an industrial school for boys, wrote about the gang activities of sixty-six boys from Massachusetts. These were not the same "street Arabs" whom we had encountered in New York City. A number of them, aged ten to sixteen, came from fairly stable families, enjoyed basketball, football, and swimming, and even went to church on Sunday, but together with their groups they misbehaved in various ways:

"C . . . gang fought with E . . . gang. We met in the middle of the ice on M . . . River. Fought with clubs, sticks, and stones. There were about four hundred of our boys and about the same number on their side. We licked. One of our fellows got knocked out. Half of us got it on the arms. The ice broke in on the river and a lot of our fellows pulled the other fellows out. . . . One little fellow on the other side got drowned.

"Stole pigeons. Broke into slot machines. Get lager beer Saturday nights off beer teams. . . . Tie a rope across the street and trip people up. Throw eggs at people. Throw cabbages at people. Ring doorbells. Break windows, electric lights. . . . Plague Jews and Italians. Tip the rag teams of Jews over. Take the rags and sell them to some other Jews . . . Have a dead rat. Throw it at Chinaman. Fire things at men to get the chase. Hit men out of doors to get the chase. Put a rock in a paper bag for men to kick."

Around 1928, when Asbury wrote about the youth gangs of his own day, he observed that they had become less criminal. But, he added, "it is quite likely that there are as many juvenile gangs in New York today as there ever have been." He reported that gang fights used to start around election-night bonfires when one gang raided the woodheaps of another "until recent years when the custom has fallen somewhat into disuse."

When fights did erupt, the weapons were wooden swords. Wash-boiler covers served as shields: "Invariably the excitement overcame them, and they resorted to bricks and stones, with the result that a few heads and many windows were broken."

In discussing delinquency and youth gangs one

should also consider the wretched slums which helped to spawn them. The most notorious of the nineteenth century slum habitations in New York was the Old Brewery in the center of the Five Points. When beer manufacturing ceased in 1837 the building was turned into a tenement. It housed more than one thousand men, women, and children. In one furnitureless room called the Den of Thieves, lived more than seventy-five people of all ages and both sexes. Many of the women were prostitutes who transacted their business right there.

By 1868, there were 18,582 slum tenements in New York City. It was estimated that about half a million people—half the city's population—lived in them. A certain block in the area between 17th and 19th streets was named "Misery Row." Brace gave this description of it:

"Here the poor obtained wretched rooms at a comparatively low rent, these, they sub-let and thus, in little, crowded, close tenements, were herded men, women, and children of all ages. The parents were invariably given to hard drinking, and the children were sent out to beg or steal. Besides, other children, who were orphans, or who had run away from drunkards' homes, or had been working on the canal-boats that discharged on the docks nearby, drifted into the quarter, as if attracted by the atmosphere of crime and laziness that prevailed in the neighborhood. These slept around the breweries of the ward, or on the hay-barges, or in the old sheds of 18th or 19th streets. They were mere children, and kept life together by all sorts of street jobs—helping the brewery laborers, blackening boots, sweeping sidewalks, 'smashing baggages' [as they called it], and the like."

Brace estimated the number of homeless and vagrant children in New York City "after long observation" at twenty to thirty thousand.

Young persons from all walks of life have a need to be accepted by their peers and to be part of a group, be it formally structured or merely a clique of some sort, and many of these groups set valor in some kind of unlawful behavior; most of us, in our adolescence, belonged to groups that fancied cheating in school, playing hookey, and so forth.

The unloved slum youngster, uneducated, unskilled, and with a low self-esteem is particularly attracted by the gangs of his neighborhood which are often the only opportunity for him to get a feeling of belonging. They also give him a sense of identity especially through their rituals, costumes, and bravado names. The norms of the gang—at odds with those of society at large— give him an opportunity for recognition through courage and cunning in acts of violence and property offenses when all the opportunities of legitimate society appear to be closed to him.

Modern social scientists have identified various types of gangs, at least two of which existed in the past. One type, perhaps exemplified by the Little Day Break Boys, was linked with adult, professional, organized crime aiming at illegal profits. Such groups frown upon violence *per se*, and resort to it only when necessary to do business. Another type, the "conflict gang," has usually no connection with organized adult crime, and exists to fight for "rep" or "turf," to commit acts of violence and vandalism, mainly for status and usually without much thought of material gain. But, as the two types are ideals, they often cannot be found in reality in pure form, e.g., many conflict gang members also steal.

To be sure, there is enough robbing and mugging in our cities today to cause alarm. Does this mean there is more crime and delinquency today than, say, one hundred years ago?

We must remember that the number of crimes increases with the population. But population growth also means growth in the number of marriages, households, automobile users, and so on. These increases do not necessarily indicate a greater *intensity* of criminal behavior.

But, have delinquency figures not grown faster than the population? True enough, if we look only at the past ten years or so. Unfortunately, reliable and useful national crime and delinquency statistics go back only that far. The few cities, such as Cleveland, that possess comparable crime statistics over a very long period show a remarkable stability over the years. They also show that today's crime and delinquency rates are far from the highest in history. Recent short-range increases in crime and delinquency may be offering a distorted picture of what has been happening over the years.

And even these short-range increases show only that more crimes (or criminals) have come to the attention of the authorities. There is again a large amount of hidden crime about which we have no statistics. To imply from the statistics for known crime that the unknown crime has also increased is often not justified. Increases in the statistics may be due to intensified policing, better record keeping and widening of the scope of the law, and—in the case of juvenile delinquency particularly—to a reduction of the tolerance of the community against certain forms of behavior.

New York City now has eight times as many inhabitants as in the days of Brace. Therefore we could expect that there would be eight times as many juvenile delinquents, merely because of the population growth. Actually we should expect even more delinquency today because we now categorize so much more misbehavior as delinquency as compared with the earlier period. Yet the New York City Juvenile Court Section of the State's Family Court disposed of only 18,545 juvenile delinquency cases in 1967, exclusive of traffic offenses.

As pointed out, official statistics do not necessarily reflect true delinquency; moreover, the number of court dispositions (in 1967) and of the estimated number of delinquents (around 1870) are not variables that can be compared statistically in the technical sense. However, the available picture certainly does not suggest a spectacular increase in delinquency over a long run.

Understandably we feel that there is more delinquency today than in the past, especially because youth crime receives so much emphasis in the news media. But we really do not know. Perhaps we can fill the gap somewhat better when we gain a deeper historical perspective on juvenile delinquency.

Homeless street children of the nineteenth century

WHEN CULTURE CAME TO MAIN STREET

by William Baker

*T*he bouncing buckboard pulled to a clattering stop at the end of the main street in a small Midwestern town. It was a hot afternoon in July, and dust swirled in from an open field where a large brown tent had been pitched. In a nearby pennant-hung booth a man in a striped shirt and straw hat leaned on the counter and riffled a stack of tickets with his thumb while he eyed the leathery-faced farmer and his wife as they got down stiffly from the wagon and plodded towards the booth.

"We'll take two of them season tickets for the whole show," said the farmer, fishing through his purse with a calloused finger. "Me and Maw spent a heap o' money educatin' our children, and now, by golly, we're glad to have a chance to spend a few dollars on our own." Clutching their tickets, they hurried across the stubbled field to the big tent where a large audience sat warm and sweaty under the hot canvas, shooing flies and fanning themselves fitfully. They'd waited all year for Chautauqua and it soon would be under way, pumping new life into their withered spirits.

This was an increasingly familiar scene in the small towns of rural America shortly after the turn of the century. The traveling Chautauqua—put together of the best elements found in the "uplift" of the original Lake Chautauqua Assembly and the glamour of the old lyceum entertainment bureaus of the Midwest—in 1903 started hustling inspiration, education, and entertainment to the isolated millions who lived on farms and in small towns across the country.

By 1924, this phenomenon of American enterprise, ingenuity, and efficiency had spread with the glittering insistence of quicksilver, raising its tents in more than 10,000 small towns in every state in the Union. Chautauqua paraded across its stages some 6,000 entertainers, musicians, speakers, actors, and politicians, who captured the hearts and imaginations of 35 million people before it suddenly died in 1925, burning out like a shooting star in the warm summer skies over rural America. But before it passed from the scene, it spent its talent lavishly and with a prodigal hand.

Even had Chautauqua been less profligate with the artists it brought with its brown tents, it still would have easily won the hearts of the audiences which crowded onto the green benches under the canvas. Less than 60 years ago, the small rural towns which freckled the face of a still-adolescent United States were made up of people who rarely ventured beyond the moat of city or county boundaries, and who lived in a stifling cocoon of provincialism. Whatever may have been considered as "culture" either had not yet reached them or detoured on its way to more metropolitan areas. Rural life was hard, dull, circumscribed, and without inspiration.

There was little that could inspire. Plays, concerts, speeches—anything that would pass for entertainment in a more formal sense was virtually unknown. Radio had not yet made its debut, and the debatable merits of television were still over the horizon. Henry Ford's ubiquitous "Tin Lizzie" hadn't yet begun to string the towns together with the tracks of its skinny wheels, and the ruts which passed for roads offered little incentive to hitch old Dobbin to the shay and go visiting.

But they hungered for something more. Music such as "Meet Me in St. Louis, Louis," was something less than moving, and the only speeches they heard were at Sunday meeting, and those usually prompted widespread nodding, more in sleep than in agreement. Reading about national and world tide of events in a week-old newspaper was a poor substitute for hearing about it from someone who had been involved, and the prospect of getting any entertainment from truly artistic performers was a dim dream or a vague hope. So when Chautauqua appeared on the scene to offer relief from tedium and inspiration for shriveled spirits, its success was immediate and spectacular.

Small wonder, then, that the staple item on any Chautauqua was the inspirational lecture which, like the Piper of Hamelin, irresistibly drew the people up Main Street and into the tents. Circuit managers referred to them as "Mother, Home and Heaven" talks, and some of the big crowd-pleasers bore such ponderous titles as "The Dawn of a New Day," "Rags and Rainbows," "Cash, Conscience, and Country," "Morals and Machinery," and "Why God Made Women."

Inspirational orators came by the dozen, and, though the early ones usually lacked a "big name," they were excellent speakers. One of the most famous, though hardly inspirational, lectures was given by a Robert J. Burdette on the weighty subject of "The Rise and Fall of the Mustache." In a period of 20 years, Burdette gave this lecture no less than 4,000 times.

The greatest single speech, at least from the point of durability, ever given on any circuit was the "Acres of Diamonds" speech by Russell H. Conwell, who later founded Temple University with most of the money he made on the Chautauqua stage. Conwell gave this speech an incredible 6,000 times at fees ranging from $100 to $500 a night in a lecturing career which spanned 40 years.

"Acres of Diamonds" had for its basic theme the power of money which could be used for good and for worthy purposes, and that people could improve their lot by discovering the riches lying all around them. He found widespread agreement among audiences when he told them they had no right to be poor.

Though much of the speech was trite, Conwell himself was anything but insincere. He had an abiding concern for worthy students trying to get a college education, and would keep a list of needy students in his pocket. After getting paid a handsome stipend for delivering his speech, he would consult the list and forward a good portion of the money to the next lucky young man.

Burdette and Conwell were in the vanguard of what was to become an impressive roster of personalities touring the circuits. As Chautauqua grew, the variety and talent of the speakers cut across all lines of interest, and the "Mother, Home and Heaven" lectures expanded into other fields—prohibition, social problems, travel, women's rights, humor—and drew such speakers as Jane Addams, Judge Ben F. Lindsey of companionate marriage renown, Sinclair Lewis, Richard Halliburton, Sir Hubert Wilkins, and Drew Pearson, whose father, Paul, managed one of the circuits.

These great, or soon to be great, names rubbed shoulders with others in the same category. Headliners on the circuits included Herbert Hoover, who talked on our duty to feed starving Europe, and Edna Ferber, Stephen Leacock, and Walter Lippman, who gave the people a look at real, live authors. Laredo Taft would sculpt a figure on stage and keep a sharp look-out for young people who might have talent that could be developed. Irvin S. Cobb—called "the funniest man on Chautauqua"—and Will Rogers invariably drew big crowds with their unique brand of humor. Winston Churchill and Prince William of Sweden lent the glamour of faraway places.

Others such as Alben W. Barkley, Robert E. (Admiral) Peary, Ruth Bryan Owen, and James Whitcomb Riley were typical attractions. An entertaining young ventriloquist named Edgar Bergen sat a wood dummy called Charlie McCarthy on his knee and directed insolent remarks at himself, and Conrad Nagel, billed as "the world's handsomest man," later became a leading motion picture star of the late 1920's and early 1930's. Lowell Thomas was using the stage to good advantage in polishing his famous well-modulated speaking voice, and John McCormack brought the green hills of Ireland to the brown fields of the circuits with his rich melodious singing.

The music which filled Chautauqua's tents wasn't limited to Irish tenors. For all the glamorous names and the "uplift" oratory which drew and held the crowds, it was music which revealed the inherent good taste which was a part of rural America. They took readily to such impressive groups as the Boston Light Opera Company, the San Carlos Opera Company, and the Chicago Grand Opera Company singers. All carried their listeners to heady heights and left them breathing a little faster in the rare atmosphere of the classics. Male quartets, harpists, bands, New England choirs, and Negro singers crooning songs of the old South brought music which moved many to the point of tears.

101

For others, the New York City Marine Band set heavy boots, plain shoes, and a few bare feet to tapping vigorously. There seemed to be no highbrows, lowbrows, and middlebrows in the matter of musical taste.

A natural antidote to the possibility of a case of cultural colic from too much of "the finer things" were the politicians who trod the hustings of Chautauqua, finding it a ready-made platform to enhance their image and further their political careers. People accepted them with good humor, tolerance, or enthusiasm, depending on the speaker and his particular persuasion. It gave them a chance to hear politics and to talk about it after the show, and provided plenty of fodder for the inevitable discussions which went on all winter in the wake of Chautauqua.

The thin stream of politicians which trickled out to the countryside grew in size until such political lights as Socialist candidate for President Eugene V. Debs, William Howard Taft, Senator George Norris, Vice-President Marshall, Al Smith, and Robert M. La Follette, the Wisconsin Progressive, all appeared at one time or another on the circuits.

La Follette was the butt of one of the standing jokes on almost every circuit on which he appeared. With the inevitable pitcher of water and glasses on the rostrum, politicians became known as one, two, or three pitcher men, depending on the length of the talk. La Follette had the impressive rating of four pitchers, and during one of his early extended talks an old farmer was heard to say in a loud voice, "By heck, it's the first time I ever saw a gas engine run on water." It followed La Follette throughout his Chautauqua appearances, causing a ripple of subdued laughter whenever he reached for the pitcher. Strangely, he never found out, but would archly inquire as to what was so unusual about a man taking a drink of water.

Overshadowing and making a runner-up of every luminary who ever appeared on Chautauqua was the greatest drawing card in the history of culture under canvas—William Jennings Bryan, "the great commoner." Bryan was Chautauqua's highest paid performer, receiving as much as $2,000 for a single lecture. He was "good for 40 acres of parked Fords anywhere, at any time of the day or night." His specialty was the moralizing lecture, and the great favorites were "Prince of Peace," "Value of an Ideal," and "The Price of a Soul."

The content of his lectures was almost lost in the brilliance of his delivery. Possessing the most magnificent speaking voice of his day, Bryan probably could have recited Mother Goose rhymes and still have kept his audience enthralled. His voice had an unusual ringing quality which could carry clearly for a distance of three blocks, and he once addressed a crowd of 10,000 people in San Francisco without benefit of mechanical amplification. On one particular tour of the circuit he gave seven speeches a day for six straight weeks without dropping a decibel in volume. His voice simply never gave out. The physical proportions of his mouth were so large that one listener was moved to remark that "That fellow could whisper in his own ear."

Chautauqua was the perfect milieu for Bryan, and while the content of his lectures failed to arouse enthusiasm in the intellectual community, they found a more than receptive audience in the small towns across the nation. Until Clarence Darrow destroyed him in the historic Scopes "Monkey Trial" in 1925, Bryan remained the greatest single attraction in the glittering history of Chautauqua.

Aside from the prodigious assortment of talent which Chautauqua employed to dispense culture, the logistics involved in just setting up and moving a show along the circuit were impressive enough to warrant mention.

In the beginning, a Chautauqua ran for five days playing five towns simultaneously. The big brown tents, specially made and a trademark of the show, were set up in each town together with green painted benches, pennants, programs, and advertising posters. Local youths or college boys in the employ of Chautauqua pitched the tents and did the hard work in the hot sun. Young ladies, school teachers, or girl scouts who were handy with children took the small fry in town and organized them into Chautauqua boosters, mainly to keep them out of the tents while the show was on.

Performances were given morning, afternoon, and evening. When the first day's show was completed, the performers started packing for a morning departure to the next town, leaving early enough to make room for the arriving next day's show. After the fifth day's show had finished, the tent in the first town was struck and moved on to the head of the line, set up, and made ready for the arrival of its first performers from the town immediately preceding. Thus, the circuit played leapfrog through a series of towns until the season ended and the bookings were completed.

A tour on a Chautauqua circuit was hard work. With the season in the North running from May until September, the weather was usually hot, muggy, fly-infested, and full of the discomforts of early-day travel. Accommodations and food often were poor, and artistic temperaments would flare. But in spite of all this, the hunger for the offerings of the performers insured an eager welcome and enthusiastic response which inspired them to give their best once on the stage. They thrived on the wild applause that usually greeted them, forgetting for a few hours the generally miserable trip that awaited them.

If life on backstage Chautauqua was short of tinsel and excitement, the face it presented to the audience was the other side of the coin. The aura of glamour surrounding the great personalities, the thrilling music and song, the speakers and joke-tellers who by now had winnowed out the clunkers and had a sparkling inventory of sure-fire crowd-pleasers—all were pulling people into the big tents in ever-increasing numbers.

Chautauqua was coming full bloom in the early 1920's. It was making more money, playing to more people, and pitching its tents in more towns every year. Its empire was spread from coast to coast, and a circuit even ventured successfully into Canada under the name of Canadian Fall Festivals. Hardly a town of any size had been untouched.

The economic effects on Main Street were incalculable—town populations would increase enormously during a Chautauqua run, leaving extra dollars in otherwise skimpy tills. During the years that Chautauqua played Merom, Indiana, population then 500, more than 100,000 individual paid admissions were recorded. The demand for the music, the "Mother, Home and Heaven" talks, and the political bombast was insatiable. It seemed that Chautauqua would go on forever. And always, as the show ended, circuit managers would hurry the sponsors in each town to sign a contract for the next year while enthusiasm ran high, thus insuring a return engagement.

Aside from the ready-made market which Chautauqua found in every small town, the contract was the greatest single factor which guaranteed its financial success. It was the backbone of the whole movement and a classic example of a "heads-I-win-tails-you-lose" arrangement.

An open-faced document, it was simple in its language, completely devoid of legalities, tricky small print, or cloudy phrases. Its meaning was stated clearly: signers of the contract guaranteed up to $2,500 to underwrite the Chautauqua, and sponsors must have half, and preferably all, of the money in the local bank

105

on opening day. Season tickets would sell at $2.50 to make up the guarantee. Each sponsor was individually liable for the whole amount or for any deficiency. The contract promised nothing but "a Chautauqua," and no mention was made of the kind or amount of entertainment. The catch in the contract was also spelled out for all to read: Season ticket sales were limited to the amount of the guarantee, and all single ticket sales went to the manager of the circuit.

And there it stood, the single ticket portion of the contract, like the Iron Maiden of Nuremberg, seeking to clasp the sponsors to her spiked bosom. A big name drawing card on a Chautauqua would sell thousands of single admission tickets at 75 cents to those not inclined to part with $2.50 for the whole show. Since the sponsors were to receive none of the single ticket sales, all that revenue flowed into the coffers of the management. In effect, the contract gave the profits to Chautauqua and the liabilities to the sponsors. It was an incredible hinge on which Chautauqua balanced as it wheeled around the country, adding ever-increasing numbers of towns to its itinerary and, even more incredible, getting the same people to sign the same document year after year.

This repetitious naivete came to a shuddering halt with a suddenness which pitched Chautauqua on its face. At the close of its greatest year in 1924, circuit managers, expecting a routine renewal of contracts, found instead to their dismay a quarter of a million sponsors across the country refusing to sign for the next year. It happened almost overnight and as if on some prearranged signal. Pencils stayed in pockets, purses remained stubbornly clasped, and heads shook negatively, like metronomes supplying a beat for the chorus of loud "noes" which answered the circuit managers' pleas to return next year. Chautauqua collapsed like one of its brown tents when the center pole was yanked, and a social phenomenon which seemingly was firmly rooted in the life of small town America was suddenly, and almost inexplicably, dead.

The sudden demise wasn't as mysterious as it seemed. True, the sponsors were the link between Chautauqua and the people, and when they failed in large numbers to sign a return contract at the end of that fatal year of 1924, it was all over. But their reasons for not signing were less obvious, though not capricious. In spite of the sponsors' apparent lack of acumen in accepting a one-sided contract, they still were shrewd enough to read correctly the changing winds that were blowing on Main Street.

For one thing, they had become acutely aware of mounting difficulties in selling season tickets, mostly because people could now get away from the farm in their new automobiles for which there were increasing numbers of relatively good roads. More significantly, they could easily travel to other towns. Also, life was getting less rigorous, creature comforts were more plentiful, and radios were beginning to vend their static-plagued entertainment in parlors around the country. The strong pull of Chautauqua as a looked-to event in what was no longer a drab, dull life was considerably lessened.

America riding away from Chautauqua on its new-found wheels could have been reason enough to write the obituary of the tent circuits, but Chautauqua itself had some built-in defects which also contributed to its downfall. The system had become so highly organized that it permitted very little, if any, deviation from planned travel dates, length of stay in town, or even subject matter of a lecture.

Speakers were required to submit copies of their speeches in advance to the management and were cautioned not to depart from the prepared script. The mass printing of programs devised to cut costs tolerated no changes of costume, act, or musical number since they were all printed in advance and the name of the particular town merely inserted at the appropriate time.

All these restrictions irked too many of the sensitive artists who found they could now stand only one trip on the circuit, leaving the show at the end of a regimented series of performances. They were replaced with inferior talents who were less sensitive, and the quality of Chautauqua began to slip. People by now knew what quality was, and the cheap carnival atmosphere which seeped in towards the last found audiences unreceptive and reluctant to buy another season ticket.

Finally, when Chautauqua music began to go downhill and the managers brought in the bird-whistlers, musical saws, and ocarina duets to replace the true artists who had fled, the last nail was driven into the coffin. When they tampered with the music, it was too much.

It was no myth that the bucolic palate was more discriminating in its tastes than it had been a quarter of a century earlier. In 1921 a string quintet became curious about Main Street taste in music and decided to play request numbers only. Keeping tabs on the most frequently requested pieces, they found that the list was headed by Beethoven's "Minuet in G," "Meditation" from *Thais*, Dvorak's "Humoresque," "Cujus Amimam" from the *Stabat Mater*, and "My Heart at Thy Sweet Voice" from *Samson and Delilah*. Musical saws could hardly compete with that, and it characterized the change in the people who had flocked to the tents for that first Chautauqua.

And changed they were. Rural Americans had been lifted from their provincialism and exposed to the music, talk, politics, and ideas which had been so conspicuously absent from their lives. They were never the same. Though Sinclair Lewis said of Chautauqua that it was "nothing but wind and chaff and the heavy laughter of yokels," this acid comment found few echoes. For all its final shortcomings, Chautauqua had truly dug the rural citizen from his cocoon of insularity by bringing him culture wrapped in canvas. Regardless of its wrappings it still was culture, and the brown tents were a turning point in the development of what is the knowledgeable, urbane, and well-informed small town of today.

Ancient Egyptian toilet case

PAINTED FACES: A HISTORY OF COSMETICS

by Brenda Gourgey

*T*he world's first pinup girl was short, fat, and, by today's standards, somewhat unkempt. She was the Venus of Willendorf and to some cavemen in around 30,000 B.C. this small limestone statue of an obese woman represented the epitome of feminine beauty—and she probably dabbed some sort of paint on her face or other parts of her body. As long ago as 50,000 B.C., Neanderthal man may have been painting and tattooing himself—first to attract the animals which provided food and later to attract women who provided comfort for him. The red ocher found in the graves of Cro-Magnon man, who followed ten thousand years later, was used as body paint and may even have served as rouge and lipstick, as it did in Ancient Egypt.

Between the Neanderthal period and the nuclear age, crude daubings have progressed to sophisticated makeup; cosmetics have been revered and reviled. Isaiah, of the Old Testament, was so incensed by the prevalence of cosmetics in his day that he raged against pretty Jewesses who used false hair and cosmetics to lure men. He warned them if they didn't cease and desist, the Lord would smite with scabs their wanton heads. Cosmetics have been equated with hell and with health; they have duped their adherents and they have even endangered their lives. But always they have survived because they are nothing more nor less than vanity in action, a compulsion as irresistible as the greed which drove men to search for El Dorado.

The Persians who curled their hair and beards into tight ringlets, the ancient Egyptians who sat at banquets with cones of perfumed oil, called nard, melting all over their bodies, were basically no different from the long-haired youngsters of today, or from those American men who, in 1968, spent $510 million on cosmetics.

The similarity is obvious between the 20th century woman who forces her hair into curls and waves with lotions and sprays, and prehistoric woman who plastered her hair with black powder and oil and twisted it into various shapes. And although in the West we may look with patronizing horror at those native tribes whose cosmetic habits are still prehistoric—who push rings through their noses, who stretch their necks and lengthen their ear-lobes—these fashions are no more extreme in principle than face lifting, scientific skin peeling, or injection of liquids to improve the bustline.

If they knew the source of some ingredients of modern cosmetics, 20th century husbands would be just as horrified as Samuel Pepys was three hundred years ago when his wife used dog urine as a face lotion, or removed superfluous hair with a mixture of cat's dung and vinegar.

However, even if the principle has always been the

same, a basic difference now is the presence of science and hygiene. For one thing, cosmetics are not as soluble as they were in the past. Elizabethan women, for example, knew only too well the truth behind the jibe in Shakespeare's *Love's Labours Lost:*

"Your mistresses never dare come in rain,
For fear their colours shall be washed away!"

With purity in a cosmetic as indispensable as whiteness in a detergent, with laws strictly regulating the ingredients, no firm today could market such a corrosive product as ceruse, or white lead, which was probably the most popular foundation of the pre-scientific age. Ceruse was used lavishly in Cleopatra's Egypt, in Ancient Rome, and centuries later in 16th, 17th, and 18th century England—despite the fact that it was known to cause scarring, pimples, headaches, dizziness, or, at worst, death from lead poisoning.

When Elizabeth I came to the English throne in 1558, a fashion boomed around her auburn hair and her ink-white complexion. Brunettes would rinse their hair in sulphur and sit in the sun for hours, enduring nosebleeds and sore eyes while they waited for it to turn gold. More often than not, the tortured locks dried up and fell out, but a century later women were still trying to alter nature and their hair was still meeting the same fate, this time from a deadly mixture of silver coins dissolved in nitric acid.

Naturally, new fashions soon appeared to conceal such calamities—masks to cover hideously scarred faces and face patches cut from black taffeta or perfumed red leather to stick over pimples and scars. Bald heads were hidden under wigs, though prices were often exorbitant, and poorer women had to resort to desperate measures. It was not uncommon 400 years ago for a child with beautiful hair to be waylaid, taken to a quiet spot, and shorn.

One of the greatest wig-wearers of the day, and the

woman who painted and powdered herself more than any other, was Queen Elizabeth herself. Her portraits show her with great mounds of tight, crimped curls for which no amount of natural hair could have been sufficient. It was quite likely that toward the end of her life, Elizabeth was bald, as was her rival Mary, Queen of Scots. At Mary's execution in 1587, her wig fell off the severed head, revealing a scalp bald except for a few wisps of grey hair.

By the 17th century, wig-wearing had once again become a fashion as well as a disguise, and a fashion for men as well as women. For example, the ill-fated Charles I, who became king of England in 1625, wore ringlets cascading down his back with a "lovelock" decorated by a ribbon thrown carelessly over one shoulder.

The Puritans, of course, thoroughly disapproved, just as today's older, more cropped generation disapproves of "hippy" hairdos and also of the increase, since about 1959, in the use of cosmetics by men. Until recently, though, these cosmetics have been invisible ones—pre- and after-shave, colognes, deodorants, talcs. Now, the recent introduction of a range of genuine make-up for men, including foundation cream and face powder, indicates that, given the present social climate and history's habit of repeating itself, the real shock is yet to come in male cosmetics.

Despite residual inequalities in some countries, Western women have, in the late 1960's, drawn roughly level with men. Careers for women, equal education, equal rights of citizenship—the suffragettes' long battle has largely been won. Except in detail, this situation has occurred before, and whenever it has, or whenever women have been dominant, men have eventually joined them in the full use of cosmetics.

Ancient Egypt, for example, had a quasi-matriarchal society with wives claiming their husbands' property and future income as part of the marriage contract. In

A Roman lady receiving her beauty treatment

addition, the painting and frescoes on the tombs of the Pharoahs show that men were practically indistinguishable from women. Both outlined their eyes with thick black kohl, both painted their eyelids green with malachite and made up their faces with ceruse, both colored lips and cheeks with red ocher. Both wore wigs, which were often colored green, gold, or blue and were made from real hair on vegetable fiber bases. Men and women alike removed wrinkles with powdered alabaster and honey, used deodorants made from incense and turpentine, and took several perfumed baths a day.

Several centuries later, certain Roman emperors were leading a similarly soft life, and a life in which women and cosmetics played prominent roles. One of the most hag-ridden was the emperor Nero, who rivaled his wife Poppaea in the depth of his make-up and carefully crimped his hair by means of a curling iron. Cosmetics in Ancient Rome were not, however, the prerogative of the emperors—one of Nero's best generals regularly refused to go into battle until he had finished applying his make-up.

In 1660, after the 11 years of Puritan austerity which followed the execution of Charles I, men were once again using cosmetics. Charles II, the restored king, was no Nero, no straw bending to the whims of strong-minded women, but he was equally self-indulgent. He was, in fact, once described as "that known enemy of virginity and chastity, the monarch of Great Britain."

In the society which took its cue from the king, the friendship of royal mistresses was an important asset at court and the first actresses began to replace boys in women's roles.

If women emphasized their power at this time with fantastic fashions—wigs rising several feet in the air, faces patched with suns, moons, stars, and crescents—

men were not far behind. In late 17th century London, it was a common sight to see men sitting in the park or theatre curling their wigs with tortoise-shell combs. To disguise spindly legs, they padded their stockings, and, like the women, they blackened their eyebrows and filled out sunken cheeks with round balls called "plumpers."

Men, too, wore face patches and the more politically minded of both sexes indicated their sympathies by patching on the left side of the face if they were Whigs (liberals) and on the right if they were Tories (conservatives).

In essence, the ribbons, lace, and velvets men wore then were no different from the flower-strewn ties, the beads, and the frilly shirts some men wear in 1969. Certainly, the "permissive society" is common to both ages, as well as to Ancient Egypt and Rome. Probably the only thing that could prevent the late 20th century from emulating former ages in the use of male cosmetics would be another age of prudery, though this, in the present moral climate, seems unlikely to happen soon.

Yet, prudery and permissiveness have been replacing each other ever since the Roman Empire finally tottered in 410 A.D., and the use of cosmetics has reflected the process. There has, of course, always been criticism of cosmetic fashions. It can be found in the works of several of the greatest literary figures of the ancient world, including Homer. The Roman poet, Ovid, who 2,000 years ago wrote a book of beauty hints for women entitled *De Medicamina Faciei*, could never resist telling how when he paid a surprise visit to a lady one morning she got so flustered that she came down to greet him with her wig on backwards.

Poets were still poking fun 1,800 years later. Toward the end of the 17th century, Matthew Prior wrote:

"Stiff in brocard and pinch'd in stays
Her patches, paint and jewels on;
All day let envy view her face
And Phyllis is but twenty-one.
Paint, patches, jewels laid aside
At night astronomers agree
The evening hath the day belied
And Phyllis is some forty-three."

This sort of thing never did, and never has, prevented anyone from using cosmetics, but the criticism which did deter was not in this witty vein.

"Whosoever do colour their faces or their hair with any unnatural colour, they begin to prognosticate of what colour they shall be in Hell!"

This daunting sentiment, as expressed by St. Cyprian, the early Christian moralist, was quoted again and again by those who equated cosmetics with the cardinal sin of pride. The disapproval of medieval preachers extended, too, to "those two-legged animals called women" whose "whorish and brothelous painting and colouring" had only one end in view—to continue the evil work done by Eve when she tempted Adam, and to drag mankind down into the abyss of sin.

Under this welter of criticism, the use of cosmetics faltered, as it did later in the Victorian age. The Victorians considered painting the face immoral, an offense against society. Women, whose lives were extremely restricted, were sternly warned that foundations—even bismuth, the most innocuous—could cause facial paralysis and, in some cases, death.

It would not be true to say that either age of prudery actually succeeded in extinguishing cosmetics altogether. What really happened was that they went underground. Those high medieval headdresses, for example, often hid elaborate arrangements of curls and braids, as well as hairlines plucked away until they reached halfway across the scalp.

The Victorians, fortunately, did not share the medieval view that washing was an evil pagan custom, and they did encourage women to care for their skin. However, it was emphasized that what they used should preferably derive from natural ingredients. This gave rise to the Victorian recipe-book of toilet preparations, an integral part of the literature of household management.

The ideas of the 17th century Puritans came somewhere between Medieval and Victorian. The Puritans were just as conscious of sin and of hell, just as certain that only by banning everything that concentrated on this world rather than the next could wretched humanity come ever near to God, but they did sanction herbal lotions made from such ingredients as cowslip, pimpernel, or the water of the elm tree.

What both Victorians and Puritans resolutely opposed was the open use of cosmetics and, in 1650, the latter even tried to introduce a bill into the English Parliament to end "the vice of painting, wearing black patches and the immodest dress of women." A similar bill, introduced as late as 1770, tried to make invalid any marriage in which the wife had lured the husband to the altar by using "scents, paints, cosmetic washes, false hair . . . and bolstered hips."

In England, both failed to get through Parliament, though the 1770 bill did become law in Pennsylvania where, as in most of the other 12 colonies, the use of cosmetics was considered brazen.

Ostensibly, all this disapproval derived from the notion that it was criminally presumptuous to try to improve God's work. However, the critics may also have realized that cosmetics virtually represented a rival religion, with the saving of beauty a substitute for saving the soul.

Quacks and charlatans rarely had any trouble mesmerising their converts and holding them to the faith.

119

Anyone, for example, who promised to wipe out the hideous scarring caused by smallpox, or remove warts and pimples, could make a fortune, however drastic their remedies.

One 17th century charlatan recommended a mixture of gold, salt, ceruse, vinegar, plantain, rosewater, and camphor which, when rubbed on the face, would make the "skin rise and fill up the hollow pits and places . . ." At this time, too, women were willing to burn their warts away with an agonizing mixture of slaked lime and lye.

If a cosmetic or treatment had the added attraction of being royal or noble, so much the better. Many 17th century women were willing to improve their complexions with the Duchess of Newcastle's remedy—burning off the top layer with sulphuric acid.

Another cure for spots was even more drastic, but sufferers willingly submitted when Dr. William Butler, physician to the heir to the throne, hung them upside down until their faces turned blue, and then cut the veins which were, he said, feeding their spots with "black, ugly blood."

Even in more level-headed Victorian times, Sarah Rachel Leverson, "Madame Rachel," was able to pull wool over many gullible eyes and charge 1,000 guineas for her "Arabian Baths" which were nothing but bran in hot water. At about the same time, a sallow-faced young woman was lured by artful advertising into buying a certain "Skin Bloom," which promised to give her complexion "the tints of the lily and the rose." "Skin Bloom" was actually a kind of enamel which set hard and was practically impossible to remove, but it is significant that the young lady used several bottles before it occurred to her that there was anything wrong.

Such implicit trust in cosmeticians, such naive hope for cosmetic miracles, would seem to need no extra incentives, but from about 1770 onwards perfume, the

la Duchesse
du Lude

The Duc de Bourgogne visiting his love,
Princesse de Sauoye, at her toilet

hidden persuader, was added first to face powder and later to most other preparations.

It has been known for centuries that perfume profoundly affects the emotions. As Oscar Wilde wrote in *A Picture of Dorian Gray:* "He set himself to discover . . . what there was in frankincense that made one mystical; and in ambergris that stirred one's passions; and in violets that awoke the memory of dead romances; and in musk that troubled the brain; and in champac that stained the imagination."

These subliminal effects were exploited fully by ancient Egyptian priests, who burned endless quantities of incense, anointed the insides of animal sacrifices, and used perfume to embalm the dead. Luscious smells also lingered about Chinese pagodas and Hindu temples. And the Greeks thought perfume was of divine origin.

However, pagans were not the only ones to recognize the psychological value of perfume. The Moslem Arabs encouraged its use when it was found to produce a state of religious ecstasy—they even put perfume in their food. As for Christians, some of their miracleworking saints were said to exhale the scent of roses when they "breathed" centuries after their death.

As in the temporal sphere, so in the secular: In India and the Far East, by far the most popular perfumes were the aphrodisiacs—musk, ambergris, patchouli, and civet—some of which are still used by perfumers today.

It seems unnecessary, then, for a manufacturer of perfumed ingredients in the cosmetics industry to enlist the help of two Americans who have studied human sexual response in order to discover which fragrances men and women find most stimulating. The answers were known thousands of years ago!

Equally superfluous seems the recent comment of a manufacturer: "The trouble is that we deal in sheer luxuries—no woman needs cosmetics." Obviously, he does not know his history, which shows that virtually throughout its whole existence, the hand that feeds the cosmetician has always had the Midas touch.

THE SUMMER ST. LOUIS PLAYED IT COOL

by Howald Baily

Americans who met at the fabulous Louisiana Purchase Exposition at St. Louis during the summer of 1904 found the weather, as usual, hot and sticky. The sweltering heat, however, did not deter thousands from converging on the Missouri metropolis to gawk and gape at the exciting sights and exhibits of that earlier out-of-this-world World's Fair. As a matter of fact, they found the heat ever so much easier to bear after their first encounter with two new-fangled "coolers" that were discovered at the Exposition—delicacies which have since become American institutions: *iced* tea and ice cream *cones*.

Long before anyone had even dreamed of the 1904 St. Louis Fair, hot tea and ice cream had been American (and world) stand-bys. Drinking tea that was iced and eating ice cream from delicious edible cones, however, were strictly innovations of the St. Louis Exposition.

There seems to be no doubt about just who was responsible for introducing iced tea; there is considerable controversy about who devised the first ice cream cone. As recently as early 1965, as we shall see shortly, the death of an elderly New Jersey man revealed him to be yet another claimant to the honor of "inventing" the cone—bringing the total to at least four persons who at one time or another have been credited as originators of the tasty ice cream container.

The earliest knowledge and use of tea per se is lost in the mists of antiquity. Some say a wise Chinese emperor brewed the first pot. Others credit its discovery to a saintly Buddhist. Whoever was first, history books and encyclopedias tell us that man has been enjoying tea for more than 4000 years. To many, life would be unthinkable without tea. It is the national drink of China, Japan, India, Ceylon, the Soviet Union, and, of course, England. Americans have been great tea drinkers since the country's earliest days, and the Massachusetts colonists even went so far as to stage history's biggest tea party in Boston Harbor back in 1773.

Although iced tea came into being in America, credit for its discovery must go to an Englishman. In 1904 young Richard Blechynden was dispatched from his Far East post to the St. Louis Exposition to popularize tea-drinking, especially the beverage brewed from his own firm's blends. The company he represented built a colorful teahouse on the fairgrounds and Blechynden set to with a will to attract visitors into his pavilion.

Day after day, however, as the city wilted under 100-plus temperatures and high humidity, the crowds passed up the Englishman's teahouse and his hot tea for other booths that might be serving something cooler. No one seemed to put any stock in the old adage that a hot drink cooled the outer surface of the body.

A New York ice cream parlor, 1870

So young Blechynden, undaunted during the early weeks of the Fair, brewed his pots of tea each morning —and poured them down the drain untasted each evening.

Whenever he had any free time—and it soon developed that was often—Blechynden strolled through the fairgrounds watching the colorful crowds milling about the awe-inspiring exhibits. One day he noted a particular booth that seemed to draw better than others, and it wasn't a "free concession" like Blechynden's teahouse. The proprietors of this booth were selling iced drinks—cups of shaved ice sweetened with fruit-flavored syrups. The young Britisher inched his way into the crowd before the counter and bought one of the drinks. It was good and it was cool. Now he had an idea.

Hurrying back to his teahouse, Blechynden ordered ice sent in and began experimenting. In no time he discovered that tea which was iced was every bit as tasty as hot tea—and certainly much, much. cooler. Now he would get the crowds into his teahouse. He soon did, and America had a new summertime drink.

The ice cream cone is another matter and its origin is not as easy to pin down. Ice cream, contrary to popular belief, is not native to this country, but dates back to Rome in the first century. Nero Claudius Caesar, emperor of Rome (54-68 A.D.), had runners bring ice from the neighboring mountains to which flavorings and fruit juices were added. So delicate was this refresher that it was served only to Nero. In time, milk was added to the ice and over the centuries the use of "iced cream" spread throughout Europe where it was especially popular with royalty.

The first evidence of ice cream in America appears in a letter written by William Bladen (1673-1718), proprietary governor of Maryland. A Mr. Hall of 76 Chatham Street (now Park Row) in New York City first advertised ice cream in this country on June 8, 1786. And George Washington had two "cream machines for ice" installed at Mount Vernon.

The first commercial ice cream factory was opened in Washington, D.C., in 1851 by an American milkman named Jacob Fussell. Five years later he expanded his operation to Baltimore and by 1864, near the end of the Civil War, the industry had spread north to Boston and as far west as St. Louis.

There were no less than 50 ice cream booths at the 1904 Exposition. Here a visitor could buy a plate of the delicious delicacy for a few pennies. Then someone—we're not sure who—"invented" the cone (or cornucopia, as it was long called) and soon fairgoers, and eventually the entire country, were demanding their ice cream in the tasty edible sugar-wafer container.

Several persons have come forward to claim the honor of being the one who first devised the ice cream cornucopia. The "official" version of how the cone and ice cream originally teamed up is this one offered by the ice cream industry: Ernest A. Hamivi, a native of Damascus, Syria, who had settled in this country, opened a concession at the St. Louis Fair where he sold a wafer-like pastry called *zalabias*. They were baked on a flat waffle iron, sprinkled with sugar and served with fruits or sweets, and were extremely popular with visitors to the Fair.

One hot day an ice cream vendor who had his booth adjacent to Hamivi's ran out of dishes. In desperation he asked his neighbor to lend him some plates. Plates Hamivi didn't have, but he suggested that perhaps by rolling a *zalabias* into the shape of a cornucopia, a scoop of ice cream could thus be served and provide customers with a two-in-one treat. On the spot Mr. Hamivi and the ice cream vendor made a deal—and America had a new gastronomic delight.

Contrary to this accepted "official" version of the

cone's origin is the contention of one Italo Marchiony, a native of northern Italy who died in this country in 1954 at the age of 86. Marchiony before his death claimed that it was he who hit upon the idea of the ice cream cone back in 1896, registering a cone-making machine of his invention with the United States Patent Office on December 13, 1903—six months before the St. Louis Fair opened. The patent read, according to Marchiony's obituary, "A model for making ice cream cups and the like." The mold was described as "split in two like a waffle iron producing several small round pastry cups with sloping sides."

Still another claim credits Charles E. Menches, a young St. Louis ice cream salesman, with the discovery of the ice cream cone. He was in the habit of taking his best girl a bouquet of flowers when calling on her. One day he showed up at her home with the usual bunch of flowers. He also had an ice cream sandwich with him that day. Lacking a vase for the flowers, his girl friend took one of the sandwich layers and rolled it into the form of a cone to serve as a vase. The other layer was similarly rolled to contain the rest of the ice cream. This version, to some at least, seems to be a rather far-fetched claim.

On February 11, 1965, an 87-year-old man named David Avayou died in Atlantic City. His obituary in the *New York Times* the next day said that Avayou, who was born in Izmir, Turkey, claimed he invented the ice cream cone while working as a laborer at the St. Louis Exposition. His story sounds remarkably like the Hami-vi version mentioned earlier, for Avayou declared that he noticed how people were eating very little ice cream at the Fair that summer because it was served on plates. To make the ice cream more palatable, Avayou claimed he devised the cone, basing his idea on the *paper* cones he had seen the French use when eating ice cream. Avayou said he carried this concept one step further by making the cone edible.

"I spent three weeks and used hundreds of pounds of flour and eggs before I got it right, but finally I found the right combination," Avayou's obituary quoted him. He first started making cones, he added, by baking them over a charcoal grill.

A Philadelphia department store hired Avayou to sell his new-found confection which had become very popular, according to the *Times* obituary. Then the store suggested that he needed a vacation, and when he returned some time later, the management, Avayou claimed, had taken over his concession and his formula, and was producing and selling its own cones.

The first commercial cone-rolling device for large-scale production—"a machine for spinning or turning a waffle"—was invented by Carl Rutherford Taylor of Cleveland and patented on January 29, 1924. No credit was given at that time to any of the several men who claimed to be the originator of the cone.

Whether it was iced tea or ice cream cones, the fact remains that by playing it cool that summer of 1904, St. Louis deserves the credit for both. Certainly the city rates the undying gratitude of an enthusiastic ice cream eating, iced tea drinking America for both ideas.

King Frederick of Prussia issued a manifesto
asking his subjects to stop drinking coffee.

THE WINE
OF ARABY

by Elenor L. Schoen

*O*n September 13, 1777, King Frederick of Prussia issued this manifesto: "It is disgusting to notice the increase in the quantity of coffee used by my subjects, and the amount of money that goes out of this country in consequence. Everybody is using coffee. If possible, this must be prevented. My people must drink beer. His majesty was brought up on beer, and so were his ancestors and his officers. Many battles have been fought and won by soldiers nourished on beer; and the king does not believe that coffee-drinking soldiers can be depended upon to endure hardships or to beat his enemies in case of the occurrence of another war."

Four years passed, and the king finally realized that he could not check the drinking of coffee. He then decided to establish a coffee monopoly and issued an edict against roasting of coffee other than in the royal roasting centers. He excepted the nobility, the clergy, and some government officials. Any application by common people for roasting licenses was refused, and the coffee-roasting license became a sort of status symbol. The poor stole their coffee or used substitutes while the king enjoyed a comfortable revenue.

This prohibition involved much conspiracy and thwarting of the law. Spies were hired to hunt down illicit coffee-roasters. This was not too arduous a job since the spy needed only to use his nose and follow the aroma of roasting coffee. People grew to hate these informers and dubbed them "the coffee-smellers."

Coffee, as the story goes, is traced back to 850 A.D. Most authorities agree that it began with a goatherd, some saying that he was an Ethiopian and others that he was an Arabian. In any case, they tell that he noticed his flock cavorting and jumping about in a strange manner. Upon investigation he saw that the goats were eating berries from a certain evergreen bush. He ate some, too. His resulting feeling of exhilaration was so great that he hastened to report the good news of this stimulating plant to one and all.

In Arabia coffee was known as *quahwah* or *bunchum* (the bean), or as "the wine of Araby." By 1475, the *Kaveh Kanes* or first coffeehouses opened in Mecca. Away from the intense heat, lawyers, students, laborers, and travelers gathered to drink coffee and listen to news and gossip from other patrons. Dozens of cups were drunk while musicians played and dancing girls entertained. Among the Turks it was customary to down 20 cups a day. And if a man failed to furnish his wife with sufficient coffee, she had an acceptable cause for divorce.

Mohammedan priests first declared that coffee was an intoxicating beverage and therefore forbidden by the Koran. Penalties were exacted from those who peristed in its use. Nevertheless, coffee became more and more popular. Early Mohammedan monks found that this drink prevented them from nodding at their meditations. They thought it proper that they should resort to this "drug of wakefulness" since the Prophet had said, "He who sleeps away half his life, lives only half his life."

Europe first learned about coffee when it was introduced to Venice about 1600. It was thought that travelers or seamen had probably brought coffee beans back to their homeland. It was first regarded as a medicine, but not for long. A coffeehouse, called a *caffe*, soon appeared, and by 1609 many such shops were serving the brew in Venice. The *caffe* was crowded with physicians, merchants, lawyers, and nobles. Ladies were frequent visitors in the evening.

Everyone did not approve of the coffeehouse and its new brew. Some condemned the *caffes* as dens of vice. Venetian priests labeled coffee an invention of the devil and petitioned Pope Clement VIII to forbid it to Christians. The Pope tried a cup and immediately pronounced it excellent. He further stated that, in his opinion, it would be a great pity if it were enjoyed only by the infidels! Then to relieve it of any evil influences he "baptized" it!

When merchants first introduced coffee to France in 1660 there was an uproar among winemakers. They attacked it as an enemy of their country whose great industry lay in the production of wine. In 1685, several French physicians praised coffee highly, saying it "countered drunkenness and nausea, relieved small pox, dropsy and gout, cured scurvy . . . and the voice benefited by well-gargled coffee."

The *Cafe de Procope*, opened in Paris in 1689, became the informal meeting place for devotees of the arts. It was reported that Voltaire daily consumed 40 cups of mocha, a drink consisting of equal parts of

A Moorish woman with her coffee and water pipe

chocolate and coffee. History relates that within these walls, Marat, Robespierre, and Danton planned the downfall of Louis XVI. Even a lowly artillery officer named Bonaparte went there to play chess. Raconteurs say that his tri-cornered hat was held in lieu of payment for his coffee bills.

Another habitue was Benjamin Franklin. Since he was such an ardent supporter of republicanism, the walls of the cafe were draped in black at the time of his death. Eventually, the coffeehouse in France offered entertainment in the form of songs, dances, and dramatic presentations. In one of these newer cafes, the famous cancan dance originated.

In Germany the coffeehouse was never as popular among the men as beer parlors and saloons. However, German women sipped "the women's drink" at their *kaffeeklatches* and liked it very well. They drank a coffee called *blumchen kaffee* so weak the pattern on the inside of fine Dresden cups could be seen through the liquid.

In 1650, according to English lore, a Jew, reputedly from Lebanon, installed the first English coffeehouse "at the Angel in the parish of St. Peter in the East," Oxford, and "there it was by some who delighted in noveltie drank." Another early English coffeehouse was one in Exeter, Devonshire, patronized by Sir Walter Raleigh. There he and his friends met to drink coffee and smoke. This was one of the first places, too, in England where tobacco was smoked.

The first coffeehouse in London, 1652, was proclaimed by its owner: "The Vertue of the Coffee drink, first publicly made and sold in England by Pasqua Rosee in St. Michael's Ally in Cornhill . . . at the signe of his own Head."

In the *Publick Adviser* on May 26, 1657, appeared this advertisement for coffee: ". . . a very wholsom and Physical drink, having many excellent vertues, closes the Orifice of the Stomach, fortifies the heat within, helpth the Digestion, quickneth the Spirits, maketh the heart lightsom, is good against Eye-sores, Coughs or Colds, Rhumes, Consumptions, Head-ach, Dropsie, Gout, Scurvy, King's Evil and many others. . . ." The advent of coffee and tea certainly brought an improvement to the breakfast beverage of previous times which had been a draught of porter or gin.

In 1663, at Marat's coffeehouse in Exchange Alley, coffee already ground with mortar and pestle could be had for three to six shillings a pound. The smell of coffee, usually described as fragrant and appetizing, was at first treated as an annoyance. A coffeehouse proprietor, James Farr, was denounced in Fleet Street for making coffee "the great nuisance and prejudice of the neighborhood."

Popularity of coffeehouses increased rapidly. They offered a brew boiled in huge pots holding from eight to ten gallons. It was usually taken black and without sugar, but occasionally some intrepid person would experiment and mix with it mustard, cinnamon, cloves, spearmint, molasses, sugar, or sour cream.

A typical coffeehouse was furnished with long, plain tables and benches. Clay pipes for smoking were usually in abundant supply. The walls might be covered with a variety of notices: an ordinance forbidding drinking liquor and using profanity, ads for complexion aids, hair tonics, quack remedies, tinctures, salves, candies, cough lozenges, plays, and auctions. Messages and letters were held for regular customers. One writer described a coffeehouse: "the whole place stank of tobacco, (with) scribbling, drinking, and arguing . . . rabble going hither and thither."

Coffeehouses were also called "penny universities" since a cup or bowl of coffee cost only a penny and a patron could listen to all manner of enlightening discussions. "So great a Universitie I think there ne'er was any, in which you may a Scooler be for spending of a Penny!" Another writer commented that "there was always much noise, much clatter, much bustle, but decency was never outraged."

Coffeehouses soon became such centers of political arguments that their influence was sometimes feared by the government. Charles II issued a proclamation on December 29, 1675, which was designed to eliminate these gathering places of dissension. "Tradesmen misspend much time (there) . . . divers false, malitious and scandalous reports are devised and spread abroad to the Defamation of his majesty's government and to the Disturbance of the Peace and Quiet of the Realm."

But Charles had not reckoned how indispensable the coffeehouse had become to the average Englishman. His populace was outraged, and voices raised a clamor all the way to the palace. Charles hurriedly and advisedly took heed. Just eleven days later he recalled his proclamation, out of "princely consideration," it was explained, "and royal compassion."

The number of coffeehouses continued to grow and by 1710 it was estimated there were 2000 in London. At the beginning, only men were admitted. Perhaps that is why the coffeehouse was attacked by the women who banded together and distributed a tract: "The Women's Petition Against Coffee, representing to public consideration the grand inconvenience accruing to their Sex from the excessive use of the drying and enfeebling Liquor." Eventually, English coffeehouses admitted women, the first being the Golden Lion in 1717. Yet coffee was sipped as a protection against the plague. And childless women drank it in hopes of conceiving, while fathers quaffed a large amount with the contrary thought that it might make them less fertile.

The Abbe Prevost who lived in London during the 1730's wrote: ". . . what attracts enormously in these coffeehouses are the gazettes and other public papers.

All Englishmen are great newsmongers. Workmen habitually begin the day by going to the coffeerooms in order to read the latest news."

Phillip Moritz recorded his observations of coffeehouses when he traveled to England in 1782. He mentioned that he often noticed groups sitting around tables and discussing in easy fashion the news of court and town. One of these groups might include a couple of lords, a baronet, a shoemaker, a tailor, a wine merchant, or others. He wrote: "The government's affairs are as much the concern of the people as of the great. Every man has the right to discuss them freely. Men condemn, approve, revile, rail with bitter invectives, both in speech and writing, without authorities daring to intervene. The King himself is not secure from censure. The coffeehouses and other public places are the seats of English liberty."

About 1630, the coffeehouses at Oxford bore the blame for the "decay of study" there. As recently as 1935, a retiring scout of Wadham college stated that "the place has never been the same since we have had women and coffeehouses." Coffeehouses, on the other hand, were preferred by many to taverns and alehouses, because there "continued sippings tho' never so warily, would be apt to fly up into their brains and render them drowsy and indisposed for business."

Gradually, each coffeehouse and its patronage began to assume individual characteristics. One such was near St. James Park where all the customers were described by Macaulay as "fops with their heads and shoulders covered with black or flaxen wigs." They all took richly scented snuff and "the atmosphere was that of a perfumer's shop."

An unusual kind of coffeehouse was that established by a barber, James Salter, in Chelsea in 1695. Vice-Admiral Munden, who was fond of Spanish titles, called the barber "Don Saltero," and so Salter called himself ever after. His place contained a museum and a coffee-house and bore a sign, "The Chelsea Knackatory," where one could see "relicks of the Sheba Queen," "fragments of Bob Crusoe," and drink coffee. Don Saltero would, if so desired, also bleed, shave, or draw teeth.

The famous Will's coffeehouse where smoking was heavy became dedicated to "polite letters, and talk was about a poetical justice and the unities of place and time." John Dryden was usually found there, and everyone contrived to be near his chair to hear his words about Racine's last tragedy or some new treatise. A pinch from his snuffbox was counted a great honor.

There were coffeehouses which were the favorite meeting places of medical men, surgeons, and apothecaries. In the Puritan coffeehouse, no oaths were heard and "lank-haired men discussed election and reprobation through their noses." There were rumors that Jesuits assembled at Popish coffeehouses, plotting and scheming over their cups and "casting silver bullets to shoot the king."

Edward Lloyd was a proprietor of a coffeehouse in Lombard Street during the reign of Queen Anne. The great insurance company, Lloyd's of London, had its beginning under this roof about 1698. Merchants and sailors met there where Lloyd had erected a pulpit for auctions and for reading out shipping news. He kept a record of ships and cargo with special emphasis on those which would most likely need insurance.

Some of the greatest prose in the history of England was probably inspired and composed in the smoky rooms of coffeehouses. *The Tatler* and *The Spectator* were possibly the later embodiment of the clever conversations of men like Dryden, Pope, Steele, Swift, Addison, and Pepys. They became in time the nucleus of social life. If a Londoner could not be located at his home or business, he was naturally sought in his favorite coffeehouse.

Barmaids were first found in the coffeehouses of Stuart and Georgian London. A shelf was built near the fire where pots of coffee, tea, and chocolate kept warm. This board was called "the bar." A writer explains that "at the bar, the good man (proprietor) always places a charming Phillis or two who invites you by their amorous glances into the smokey territories, to the loss of your sight." Concerning the barmaids, Steele said, "These Idols sit and receive all day long the admiration of the Youth." Some coffeehouses began to serve wine and liquors, and this seemed to mark the beginning of their degeneration. The famous coffeehouses of England slowly developed into private clubs.

Many of the early settlers in the New World already knew of coffee. Captain John Smith wrote in his *Travels and Adventures* in 1603 that the best drink of the Turks was "coffa from a graine they call coava." Coffeehouses appeared in New York, Boston, Baltimore, and Philadelphia, but they compared unfavorably with their colorful and stimulating European counterparts.

Most of the colonists viewed hours spent in these early inns as idle and, therefore, sinful. There was much work to be done with no hours to be wasted in drinking coffee and merely talking. A majority of the men disdained innkeeping as women's work. So the first license to sell coffee in Boston was assigned to a Dorothy Jones in 1670.

One of the most renowned coffeehouses of New England was the Green Dragon in Boston. British officers and local gentry mingled there. Coffee, wine, rum, and apple brandy were served. Daniel Webster referred to it as the headquarters of the revolution, where colonists like John Adams, James Otis, and Paul Revere conferred.

Coffeehouses in New York attracted merchants and the military as well as some unattached women. Wives

A German coffee house of about 1850

criticized coffeehouses because they suspected that their curtained booths might conceal some dealings other than politics or business. The Kings Arms was an outstanding New York coffeehouse; public trials and political meetings were held upstairs.

The most famous of all was the Tontine Coffeehouse opened in New York in 1792 at Wall and Water Streets. The Tontine was organized and owned by 157 businessmen. Board and lodging were provided on some of the upper floors. Its largest room was occupied by the New York Stock Exchange. The names of ships entering and leaving the port were posted; every sea captain arriving in New York would always visit the Tontine.

But the Boston Tea Party dated the real rise of coffee drinking in America. The unhappy colonists banned everything British or even suggestive of the British. Dutch and French traders rushed to provide coffee at reasonable prices. In 1808 the Exchange coffeehouse was built in Boston. It was considered to be the world's largest and most expensive. The seven story "skyscraper," modeled on Lloyd's of London, cost $500,000. There were banquet halls, sleeping rooms, and a trading center. Ship and insurance brokers, navy officers, and numerous seamen streamed into its doors. It was razed by a disastrous fire in 1818.

There have been many debates over coffee, its faults, its virtues. In July of 1911, the *Tea and Coffee Journal* quoted a Dr. Jonathan Hutchinson as saying that coffee "prevents headaches and fits the brain for work, that tea and coffee preserve the teeth, keep them in place, strengthen the vocal cords and prevent sore throat . . . have right to rank as nerve nutrient."

Advocates of drinking coffee boast that it is "good for the heart," "enhances the circulation," is "non-habit-forming," "induces sleep," is "valuable for athletes," "builds up resistance to noise," and is "completely harmless when used in moderation."

Their opposition contends, however, that coffee causes sleeplessness, a tendency to heart disease, a dependence on its stimulation, and tenseness and irritability.

It is interesting to listen to a group of people debating the proper preparation of coffee. One man will discourse learnedly that the essential element is the cleanliness of the pot. Another will lecture on the type of care of filters. They will dispute the worth of competing brands. Thoughts will be exchanged on the length of cooking time, the grinding of the bean, the use of salt and eggshells, or the kind of vessel that produces the best coffee.

One senses that this is no light matter since it concerns, obviously, the vital juice of sustenance. Brewing of coffee takes on the aspect of a religious liturgy with the preparation of the sacrifice. It is much more than a "cup of comfort." Perhaps this is the cup of desperation, instead.

But the "wine of Araby" is drunk the world over and probably always will be as long as it is made according to the recipe of Charles Maurice de Talleyrand Perigord (1754-1838): "Black as the devil, hot as hell, Pure as an angel, sweet as love."

A SHORT HISTORY
OF NURSERS

by Richard Merrill

*I*n this enlightened age the practice of breast-feeding an infant carries no social stigma, and extreme care in matters of cleanliness of utensils used in the care and feeding of babies is a matter of course. But such was not always the case. Where most primitive women breast-fed their children until they were two or three years old, the practice was looked down upon in many of the more civilized societies of the past. The wet nurse was a common household servant in ancient Egypt and again in the 13th century. Wet nurses were so fashionable in France about the time of the French Revolution that there was actually a "bureau for placing nurses" whose milk had first been tasted by the bureau's own doctor.

Until about a hundred years ago the weaning of an infant created a very difficult problem, one somewhat more complicated than finding a suitable wet nurse. The utensils used to feed the weaned child were roughly made and almost impossible to keep clean—that is if the mother was inclined to cleanliness, and a look at the infant mortality rates prior to this century would suggest that few of them were.

The first dishes for feeding babies were probably made of an oval-shaped segment of bark from a tree chipped by a flint axe. The Australian aborigines still use the bark of the eucalyptus tree. Later, pottery nursers (complete with pottery nipples) were used which were not only almost impossible to sterilize but must have been an extremely uncomfortable experience for the infant at mealtime. One of the oldest nursers still in existence was excavated in London and dates back to the Roman period. Actually it is more "modern" than some of the nursers used in this country a little over a hundred years ago. The Romans, who imported pottery and also set up kilns for its manufacture in all the countries occupied by their troops, at least concerned themselves with the child's comfort. They shaped the nipple so a child could feed with some ease.

Actually later English feeding bottles, including several from the Tudor period that have been dug up in London, show a similarity to the early Greek and Roman types.

By the time American pioneers struck out across the mountains to settle the heartlands of this country, pewter nursers, or nursers made of other metals including silver, were available, but only in the large cities and among the wealthy. The pioneer mother still had to make do with what she had, either dishes made of bark or, taking a cue from her Indian neighbors, pottery.

Mothers watched friendly Indian squaws feed their papooses and learned which new and unusual foods would sustain their babies. In Maine it was the plentiful codfish; in Kentucky it was ground corn meal or a mash of vegetables. When the corn meal supply grew short, mothers mixed it with water and ground walnuts —and nursed the baby by dipping a piece of cloth in the mixture. Colonists were always looking for better and easier ways of doing old tasks. Babies can be fed semi-solid foods with a conventional spoon, but an ingenious craftsman put a cover on the spoon so food could not be knocked out.

In England, in the second half of the 1800's, some parent concerned with a baby's comfort thought of using a bit of leather or chamois loosely stitched together in the shape of a glove finger as a nipple. A sponge was inserted in the nipple to prevent its collapse, and the infant sucked the milk through the spaces between the stitching.

The Japanese had already devised a nurser that not only was as comfortable as anything in use in the Western world but, made of white porcelain, was much easier to keep clean than the cumbersome pottery or metal nursers of England and America. The Japanese nurser contained a central well for hot water so the food in the outer tubular container could be kept warm.

Nursers of one type or another were developed by every ancient society; they have been found in the ancient Indian mounds of the Mississippi valley and Oklahoma as well as in excavations of ancient cities of the Middle East. Oddly enough, many nursers from different societies of different ages are quite similar.

In the 1800's glass became cheap and nursers made of glass replaced the hard-to-sterilize pottery and metal bottles. With the transparent glass, mothers could easily recognize that daily washing—considered the height of cleanliness with pottery feeders—was not sufficient. By 1870 rubber nursing nipples were available, and infant feeding devices began to look something like they do today.

RUB A DUB DUB: A SHORT HISTORY OF HOME LAUNDRY

by Ronald Leal

*I*t would have happened a few years after 1184 B.C. As told by Homer in *The Odyssey*, Nausicaa, the princess of the Phaeacians, approached the king one morning with a petition:

"Father dear, couldst thou not lend me a high waggon with strong wheels, that I may take the goodly raiment to the river to wash, so much as I have lying soiled? Yea, and it is seemly that thou thyself, when thou art with the princes in council, shouldst have fresh raiment to wear. Also, there are five dear sons of thine in the halls, two married, but three are lusty bachelors, and these are always eager for new-washen garments wherein to go to the dances; for all these things have I taken thought."

No father would refuse such an offer, and Nausicaa with her handmaidens was soon on the road to the river:

"Now when they were come to the beautiful stream of the river where truly were the unfailing cisterns, and bright water welled up free from beneath, and flowed past, enough to wash the foulest garments clean, there the girls unharnessed the mules . . . Then they took the garments from the wain, in their hands, and bore them to the black water, and briskly trod them down in the trenches, in busy rivalry. Now when they had washed and cleaned all the stains, they spread all out in order along the shore of the deep, even where the sea, in beating on the coast, washed the pebbles clean. Then having bathed and anointed them well with olive oil, they took their mid-day meal on the river's banks, waiting till the clothes should dry in the brightness of the sun."

This most poetic of laundry stories exists because at this point Homer tells that the shipwrecked Odysseus came out of hiding to present himself to the princess in the hope of getting a new start toward Ithaca. Although considered only legend, Homer's *Odyssey* has been proven by modern archaeological research to represent accurately the customs of the age, and the story provides in vignette a pretty picture of the way laundry was done during the Golden Age of Greece.

Laundry belonged to history long before Nausicaa washed her clothes in the Phaeacian river, however. Even before what we call the dawn of civilization in Egypt and Mesopotamia, the lake dwellers were wearing and washing clothes. Crude drawings left by that earlier civilization depict primitive people beating fabrics on rocks in streams.

Linen, commonly worn by the Egyptians and Phoenicians, was known 50 and 60 centuries before Christ. Evidence of weaving is found in the Khirokitia culture of southern Cyprus some 5,500 years B.C., predating the making of pottery. Cotton, first grown in India, was

Doing the laundry, circa 1890

used long before the Christian era. In the Orient, the silkworm has been raised commercially since the legendary date of 2700 B.C. Wool was used to make the clothing of both ancient Greeks and Romans.

The Egyptians were probably the first of the accomplished launderers. By the time the pharaohs started building the pyramids at Sakkara about 3000 B.C., their subjects probably were accustomed to wearing linen clothing, freshly washed and bleached in the sun. A picture of two figures washing clothes was found in the tomb of Beni Hasson, who lived about the time of Osirtasen, pharaoh in the 18th century B.C. who is thought to have invited Jacob to Egypt to settle down in Goshen.

Egyptian women took their washing to the banks of the Nile, used sticks, paddles, and stones to free the dirt, and forced running water through the fabric. They were aided by a natural purifying agent—an earthly alkali called *niter* or *natron*—found in the Egyptian soil which they used much as soap would be used later. Sand, ashes, and soapwort root were used similarly in other parts of the ancient world. The Greeks, and later the Romans, used earths to clean many woolens that would have been spoiled by washing in water.

The Phoenicians carried the methods of the Egyptians into the south of Gaul—now France—a half-dozen centuries before the birth of Christ, and it was from the Gauls that the Romans learned of them. In A.D. 70, Pliny the Elder wrote that the Gauls boiled goat tallow with a liquid drawn from beechwood ashes (lye), but they used it as a hair pomade, not as a cleanser. It was the Greek physician Galen who first observed that his Gallic mixture was an effective cleanser.

A similar form of soap was discovered in the earth on Sapo Hill, outside Rome, sometime prior to 200 A.D. A legend tells that the melted fat from the sacrificial animals mixed with wood ashes from the fires and was washed down into the clay. The women of the place used the clay in washing their clothes. It is generally accepted that the word soap comes from *Sapo*.

Through all these early discoveries, most women continued to wash clothing with only water and their own energy. The Gallic mixture was too expensive; Sapo clay was too rare. It was not until the ninth century, when the Arabian alchemist Ibn Hajan Dschabir compounded the first known soap formula, that soap gained wider use in washing clothes. The first great centers of the soap industry grew at Marseilles in France, Savona in Italy, and Castile in Spain.

With or without soap, washing clothes was a regular part of all early civilizations, although Nausicaa is the only princess we know of who washed her own clothes. Washing involved beating, trampling, and soaking the fabrics in running water with variations only in the kind of stick or rock used.

The importance given cleanliness in the early societies often came from religious codes. Egyptians cleaned not only their own clothes, but also those of idols representing the spirit *ka*, whom they believed to share their existence. The *Vedas*, sacred Hindu books, established washing of clothes as essential to physical and moral well-being. In the laws given by Moses to his people, cleanliness was a sign of religious purification. He decreed that if clothing could not be cleaned by two washings, it was unclean in the moral sense and was to be burned. Among the Aztecs of pre-Columbian Mexico and several other early American Indian societies, cleanliness was a matter of law. To go about with unclean clothing or body subjected one to the death penalty.

After the fall of Rome, however, cleanliness became suspect. The Christians associated the luxury with paganism. By the 7th century, washday in Europe was a

From the time of Princess Nausicaa (1184 B.C.)
until J. Breton made the above painting in 1892 A.D.
laundry methods changed very little.

twice-a-year function for the entire village. It was not, ironically, until the knights began to return from the Crusades that the importance of cleanliness was restored. The Christians relearned cleanliness from the subjects of Mahomet, who commanded all Moslems to keep their clothes and bodies clean.

Still it was a luxury. During the Middle Ages, the masses of people gave little importance to cleaning their clothing. The same was true during the Renaissance, which was otherwise a period of enlightenment. Strong perfumes took the place of cleanliness in many silks and velvets worn by lords and ladies. Most people clothed themselves in wool and seldom washed it.

New laundry methods were slow to develop. At the beginning of the 19th century, methods used by the Greeks 30 centuries earlier were still in use. The English fullers—professional launderers—used lye, ammonia, and fuller's earth; soap was still too expensive. Then French scientist Nicholas Leblac found that soda ash, one of the most essential raw materials in soapmaking, could be extracted from common salt. Soapmakers then had a plentiful supply of vital material and were no longer dependent on wood ashes. For the first time soap became available at a reasonable cost.

Meanwhile, in England, laundry's first mechanical aid was put to use by professional fullers. They found a way of trampling fabrics with machines rather than doing it with their feet. Another important development of the early 1800's was the introduction of the wash boiler, which came into use in both Europe and America.

Laundry through all its ages has been primarily the work of women. When Florence Nightingale went to the Crimea to nurse wounded troops in the middle of the last century, she made laundry the first task for herself and her nurses.

The prospectors in the California Gold Rush, outnumbering the women 12 to one, sometimes sent their shirts all the way to China to be laundered. Frontier housewives used grease from their cooking and wood ashes from their fires to make their own lye soap. They worked with wooden washtubs and scrubboards and—following a custom established by the Pilgrims at Plymouth Rock—made Monday washday an institution in the American way of life.

In 19th century America, the homemaker who followed popular washing instructions of the time would rise early on Monday morning and spend the day in approximately the following manner:

She built a fire in the backyard and heated a kettle of water—most likely rainwater—while taking care to arrange her washtub so that smoke would not blow into her eyes if the wind was strong.

She shaved a whole cake of lye soap into the water after it began to boil.

She sorted her soiled clothing into three piles—white, colored, and heavy pieces such as work clothes and rags.

She stirred flour in cold water, thinned it with boiling water, and used it to rub dirty spots, holding the clothes against a board. She boiled the white things; the colored clothings were scrubbed by hand, wrung out, and often starched with a mixture of flour and water.

She removed her white items with a broomstick, wrung them out by hand, and treated them with bluing and starch.

She hung the clothes out to dry, and perhaps used the hot soapy water to scrub her porch afterward.

And then she rested. Ironing was reserved for Tuesday. It was just as complicated and, possibly, even more work.

Only ladies of wealth and high position avoided the ordeal of Blue Monday. One so fortunate was the nation's first First Lady. Martha Washington's washing was done by two servant women who were assisted by teenagers. The laundry at Mount Vernon might be called the ideal laundry center of early America.

The washhouse is a one-room wooden building covered with cypress shingles, occupying about 16' by 24' of floor space. It is lighted by two small windows, with doors opening to a drying green or laundry yard. A brick fireplace and a brick masonry stove, which holds a copper cauldron, are the only stationary articles in the room.

An inventory of the contents of the washhouse, taken by the executors of General Washington's estate, listed nine tubs, four pails, two piggins (small wooden pails with extended handles), four tables, two boilers, and one wooden horse—an extravagant collection of washing equipment for those early days. Irons were kept elsewhere. In those days only ironing was known as "laundry." Washing was simply washing.

A frontier housewife would have thought the Mount Vernon arrangement one of unimaginable luxury. There was no Monday washday for Martha Washington. She therefore predated the end of this unbeloved tradition by 150 years. Not until the middle of the 20th century would American homemakers cease to associate Monday with washday and instead do their laundry with ease any day of the week.

In 1780 an Englishman named Rodger Rodgerson filed for a patent on a new invention " an entirely new machine called a laundry for the purpose of washing and pressing of all sorts of household linen, wearing apparel, and other things, in a much less expensive and laborious and expeditious manner than any hitherto practiced."

This patent was the apparent starting point for the profusion of washing mechanisms that began to appear in the early 19th century. It probably gave the term "laundry" the definition it commonly has today.

In France and Germany, as well as in England, similar ideas were being developed even as Rodgerson filed his patent. And in the United States one Nathaniel Briggs was issued a patent on March 28, 1797, for a device to be used in "washing cloaths."

All these early machines were friction devices, although they varied in construction. Their mechanical components, whose names—the kicker, dasher, beetle, cradle, dolly, poser—have become part of American folklore, were meant to do mechanically what the ancient Egyptians had done by hand—to beat, rub, and mash dirt out of clothes.

For example, a washer patented in the United States in 1805 was composed of a tub, a corrugated board, and a lever. It offered no easy operation. Dirty clothes were put into the bottom of the tub. The board with the lever attached was pressed on top of the clothes. The operator then pulled the lever back and forth in an irregular, jerky motion, rubbing the clothes against the corrugated bottom.

Some washers used tubs made of half-barrels and corrugated bottom-boards made of wagon-wheel spokes. Another type featured a large corrugated roller with four small rollers beneath fashioned to revolve as they met the grooves of the larger roller, rubbing the clothes as they went through. Some were turned by cranks; others played back and forth as the machine rocked on a "cradle" or turned about.

Innovations were many and varied. The Cataract washer, created in 1831 by John Schull, consisted of two concentric cylinders, one outside the other. According to his patent, water entered "an outer cylinder constructed so as to be watertight" while the "open cylinder (was) made to revolve on gudgeons."

After Schull's washer came such variations as the Continental Washing Machine model, said to "wash a single collar or any amount of small articles up to a bulk of two or three sheets," and the Housewife's Darling, which was advertised as having only one moving part with an action that rubbed and squeezed the fabric "without any strain."

A carpenter named Charles Matee applied power to laundry in 1851, gaining credit for the nation's first motor-operated washing machine. He bought a 10-horsepower donkey engine from a ship captain, attached it to a 12-shirt machine, and made it work.

In 1863, Hamilton Smith made a successful departure from the friction principle by devising a reciprocating mechanism to reverse the movement of the revolving drum in a washing machine. The belt-driven rotary washer tumbled the clothes inside the cylinder, splashing them in soapy water.

The 19th century was the inventor's era in the development of a practical washing machine. By 1875 experiments of great and small importance had produced almost 2,000 patents for mechanical washers.

At the turn of the 20th century an electric-powered washer, operating on Smith's principle of a rotating and reversing cylinder, was introduced. During the same period the first quantity production of washers—hand-operated machines such as the Pastime and the Hired Girl—was begun. In 1914 a washer powered by a gasoline engine went on the market, providing machine washing where electrical power was not yet available—in the larger part of the nation's farm community.

The success of such developments cemented the foundation of a new industry. Manufacturers of washing machines became almost as numerous as were newspapers in that colorful era just preceding the modern age. Hundreds of models of power washers were made available to American homemakers of the early 20th century.

In 1910 a patent was issued for the swinging, reversible wringer, providing a model for wringer washers that has endured to the present day.

And in 1922 came the industry's most important invention. Howard Snyder of the Maytag Company devised a method for creating strong water currents within the tub to perform the washing action. He designed a circular plate with four vertical fins, placed it in the bottom of the tub, and attached it to a drive shaft, providing an oscillating action. This agitator quickly rendered obsolete the dolly which had been attached to the underside of the lid to pull the clothes through the water.

The impact of the innovation was immense. Within two years the Maytag Company, a small regional manufacturer in Newton, Iowa, became the leader in the industry. The groundwork was laid for large national manufacturers to replace the vast network of small, machine-shop operations that were then marketing washers to the public. And this, consequently, resulted in the availability of lower-priced, better washing machines.

This was the change that brought the laundry appliance industry into the modern age. Now, almost 50 years later, Snyder's invention, or an adaptation of it, is used almost universally in the manufacture of wringer and automatic washers. Today the average housewife can do her laundry in a fraction of the time it took Nausicaa, princess of the Phaeacians—and with a lack of effort the princess would have thought miraculous.

A *sentimental valentine from about 1850*

A SHORT HISTORY
OF VALENTINES

by Robert McCarter

*I*n the Roman calendar, St. Valentine's Day falls on February 14, and tradition decrees that folks of both sexes "exchange missives and epistles, either of comic or sentimental nature, in which the foibles of the receiver and the love of the sender are set forth in prose, verse, and emblematic picture."

No earthly reason for this custom can be traced to the two good saints whose names are made to endorse this holiday. Of the two, and possibly three, the most famous was a priest of Rome who is inaptly called the "Lovers' Saint." He wrote no love songs, nor was he ever rumored to cast a glancing eye at tender and youthful Roman maidens. But he did stand steadfast to the Christian faith during the Claudian persecutions and was stoned and beheaded for his trouble in 270 A.D. What was left of him was entombed in the church of St. Praxedes in Rome, near a gate named for him many years after, *Porta Valentini*, or Gate of Valentine.

Another St. Valentine lived in Terni in Italy and was the bishop who cured a son of Craton the rhetorician and later choked to death on a fishbone. In Italy and Germany many pray to him to cure epilepsy. Neither St. Valentine was inclined to the sweet joys now honored in celebrating the day named for them.

In 1807 the antiquary Francis Douce, writing in his *Illustrations of Shakespeare,* suggested that Valentine's Day is the Christianized form of the classic feast of Lupercalia held in Rome during the month of February in honor of Pan and Juno. Among other ceremonies, it was customary to place names of maidens in a box or urn from which they were drawn by young men. In 496 A.D. Pope Gelasius changed the Lupercalia festival from February 15 to February 14 and named it St. Valentine's Day.

In his *Lives of the Saints,* Alban Butler explained that bishops of the early Christian church worked most "zealously to eradicate the vestiges of pagan superstition; chiefly by the simple process of retaining the ceremonies, but modifying their significance." To that end Gelasius insisted on names of saints being placed in the drawing box instead of those of young girls.

Somehow this new idea found little favor with the participants in the lottery, and the balloting went back to something more akin to the original pagan ideas. Wanton youth may not have been satisfied to take a risk on a ghostly partner in heaven. Again in the 16th century, however, St. Francis de Sales once more tried to sanctify the rites of St. Valentine's Day by replacing names of eager youth with those of saints young people would do well to honor. This was the last of the influence of the sedate personalities of these two St. Valentines, however, as it lasted briefly, and no prominent church member again tampered with the tried and true pagan custom.

There is another equally reasonable theory why lovers exchange tokens on February 14. This was a belief held in Europe in the Middle Ages that the birds began to mate on this day. Chaucer, in his *Parliament of Foules*, refers to it thusly: "For this was Seynt Valentine's Day. When every foul cometh ther to choose his mate." In Derbyshire in England, young lasses followed a ritualistic procedure which echoed this belief in the 17th century. On St. Valentine's Eve, if the young lady wished to divine who her future husband was to be, she went to the local churchyard at midnight. When the clock struck 12 she began to run around the church 12 times, repeating without stopping: "I sow hempseed, hempseed I sow. He that loves me best come after me now." At the twelfth round, with any luck, her lover appeared before her.

By this time many different beliefs and strange behavior had sprung up about Valentine's Day. Samuel Pepys wrote in his *Diaries* that in 1664 he called at a friend's house but would not enter until the servant Mingo assured him he was not a woman. For the notion was the first person of the opposite sex seen on the holiday was one's Valentine.

There came to be an element of choice, though. The next Valentine's Day Pepys records that a Will Bower came to be his wife's Valentine, "she having (at which I made good sport to myself) held her hands all the morning, that she might not see the painters that were at work gilding my chimney-piece and pictures in my dining room."

Amusingly enough, however, Pepys' most rambling writings about Valentine's Day concern his urge to account in full the exact amounts of British pound sterling laid out. For it was also the custom for men to present a lady or child with a present after they had claimed him their Valentine.

It may have been this matter of out-of-pocket expense which finally led males to find equally illogical reasons for Valentine's Day. The etymologist made a couple tries. The letters *v* and *g*, for example, were frequently interchangeable in common English speech. Gallant and valiant both spring from the Latin *valens*. The Norman word *galantin*, which referred to a lover of the fair sex or what today could be laughingly called a masher, was frequently written and pronounced *valantin* or *valentin*. A conclusion could be drawn that a natural confusion of terms resulted and this was how the Sts. Valentine come to be patrons of sweethearts and lovers.

Another lover of words found his answer in the Egyptian tongue. Considering that *Va* or *Fa* meant "to bear," that *Ren* was "the name" or "to name," and *Ten* was "to determine," he concluded that Va-len-tine had nothing whatever to do with any Christian saint and referred instead to the lottery principle of choosing mates' names.

Shakespeare, who alluded to the mating of birds in February in *Midsummer Night's Dream,* demonstrated another Valentine custom in *Hamlet* when Ophelia sang: "Good morrow, 'tis St. Valentine's Day, All in the morn betime, And I a maid at your window, To be your Valentine." Common throughout Elizabethan England was the notion the first man seen by a maid from her window St. Valentine's morn would be her own true love.

Perhaps Cupid himself, the god of love Eros, has had the last say as his childlike image still graces Valentine cards—in the same way he is supposed to be embracing Psyche on Mount Olympus. There is an old tale that the first St. Valentine cured the blindness of his jailer's daughter. Cupid, with his bow and arrow, was always mischievously frolicking with another kind of blindness altogether, and perhaps this mystical wish-fulfillment is the real answer to Valentine customs throughout history.

Whatever the explanation, Valentine cards have been around long enough to instigate the custom of sending greeting cards at Christmas and the New Year. And they give penetrating glimpses of how people acted during different epochs. Many present-day cards still copy the famous children designs of Kate Greenaway in the late 19th century. And the "Penny Dreadfuls" of the same period can be contrasted to the lacily sentimental German cards produced around the turn of the century.

No longer do most women of any age blush deeply upon receipt of a Valentine card, but there was a time not long ago when these were considered true declarations of love, and many a Valentine has been—and occasionally still is—pressed into a memory book.

A multicolored cut glass cup, probably Persian,
from the ninth century

A HISTORY OF GLASS

By Ronald Leal

*T*he moon is not, as stated in the old folk tale, made of cheese, it is made of glass! Not entirely, of course, but scientists studying the contents of the receptacles that the crew of Apollo 11 brought back from last summer's moon landing have found a surprisingly high percentage of glass.

The moon glass, like natural earth glass, was fused by volcanic action. Chemically, it is very similar to manufactured glass. The most common natural glass is obsidian which is found in most parts of the world. There is an entire mountain of it in Yellowstone Park.

Obsidian is usually black but is found in other colors, including the pinkish glass from which the Aztec Indians of Mexico made their ceremonial sacrificial knives. Usually translucent, obsidian can be chipped and flaked to make a variety of implements, including arrowheads, spears, and even razors. Man was probably making tools of this natural glass as long ago as 75,000 B.C. By around 25,000 B.C. he was fashioning obsidian into a variety of objects, examples of which are exhibited in museums all over the world, and, in time, was using the material for mirrors, jewelry, and ceremonial objects.

It is not known when or where man first started manufacturing glass. The Roman historian Pliny tells us that a group of Phoenician sailors discovered how to make glass when they moored their ship on the banks of the Syrian river, Belus, under the banks of Mount Carmel. In preparing their evening meal the Phoenicians set their cauldron on blocks of niter of soda. The heat of the fire fused the soda with the sand of the river bank which resulted in a stream of liquid that poured from under the cauldron. The next morning the stream had chilled into glass. As it is highly unlikely that a cooking fire could have generated enough heat to fuse true glass, we must look upon Pliny's tale with a certain amount of skepticism.

However, we do know that man knew how to make glass at least four thousand years ago—long before he had learned how to smelt iron. It is generally presumed that Egypt was the birthplace of man-made glass but, while many conditions existed in ancient Egypt favorable to the manufacture of glass, no traces have been found of a glass industry there in the rudimentary condition. The earliest specimens of glassware found in Egypt are elaborate in detail and far in advance of the experimental period.

The manufacture of glass was probably discovered by Mesopotamian (or possibly Egyptian) potters accidentally while firing their wares. The first man-made glass was in the form of a glaze, a mixture of sand and minerals heated and fused onto the surface of stone or ceramic objects heated in an oven, producing a hard,

Line drawings of a glass factory from Denis Diderot's "Great Encyclopedia," published in 1751. Courtesy Corning Glass Works

shiny outer covering. Later it was discovered that if the glaze was thick enough, it would stand by itself. Such objects were the first man made of solid glass. The Corning Museum of Glass owns a string of Egyptian beads, dated before 1500 B.C., which contains both ceramic and solid glass. About this time the Egyptians began making small vessels and flattened bottles by dipping a sand core into molten glass. Glass threads were applied while the glass object was still hot, usually in a zig-zag pattern to give the jars and bottles striking beauty.

In Greco-Egyptian and Roman times the glass industry flourished in Egypt and all kinds of vessels were being fashioned. Glass-blowing had been invented and objects were being made both by this method and with the use of molds. Both molding and cutting were utilized as decoration. By this time the Egyptians were also particularly skilled in the manufacture of mosaic glass, which was formed by the union of rods of various colors in such a manner as to form a pattern. Mosaics were being used on buildings and to decorate caskets and furniture.

Remarkably, there was very little basic change in the constituents fused to make glass until modern times. Roman glass manufactured during the lifetime of Christ contains almost the same materials in the same proportions as soda-lime glass used in today's soda water bottles. Until the seventeenth century, the only real advance in the manufacture of glass was in the selection and purification of the materials.

While they did not change the components used in the manufacture of glass, the Romans remarkably perfected the art of glassmaking by careful selection and purification of materials, and reached a point of excellence which, in some respects, was not excelled until the last century. The Romans used glass for pavements and in thin plates for coating walls. At the time of the

A seventeenth-century German enameled armorial beaker. Courtesy The Corning Museum of Glass

decline of the Roman Empire, the Romans were manufacturing glass for windows and were in the rudimentary stage of using it for optical instruments.

As all art, that of glassmaking deteriorated during the decline of the Roman Empire.

Some of the Roman glassmakers, no doubt, migrated to Constantinople. The art was practiced there to a great extent during the Middle Ages. When Justinian erected St. Sofia he had vaults covered with mosaics and immense windows filled with plates of glass fitted into pierced marble frames. Pierced silver discs were suspended by chains to support glass lamps. Glass for mosaics was also made and exported.

In the eighth century, when peace was made between the caliph Walid and the emperor Justinian II, the former stipulated for a quantity of mosaic for the decoration of a new mosque at Damascus, and in the tenth century Constantinople mosaic for the decoration of the niche of the kilba at Cordova was furnished by Romanus II.

Glassmaking flourished under the Saracenic regime in Alexandria, Cairo, Damascus, and other cities. Glass vessels manufactured in Damascus were prized both in England and France during the fourteenth century. It was under the Saracenic influence that the processes of enameling and gilding were perfected.

As the Middle Ages drew to a close, to be replaced by the age of the Renaissance, there was a rebirth of all the arts in Europe. By 1268 glass workers had become an incorporated body in Venice and thereafter the manufacture of glass objects spiraled. In 1291 the glass factories were moved to the island of Murano to eliminate the danger of fire and to protect the secrets of Venetian glassmaking. The glassmaker who tried to emigrate or to export scrap glass could be punished by heavy penalty, even death.

By such stringent supervision of its glass industry,

In partnership with electricity, glass illuminates cities.
Courtesy Corning Glass Works

Venice was able to hold a monopoly on the production of fine glass for almost three centuries. Windows, mirrors, beads, bottles, bowls, and goblets of every description were exported to all of Europe and the Near East. The process of enameling had been imported from Damascus, gilding was freely used, and the Venetians had already devised many of the intricate ornamental processes such as the beautiful *"vitro di trina"* or lace glass.

The highest perfection of Venetian glassmaking, both in form and decoration, was reached in the middle of the sixteenth century. But England and France had gradually acquired knowledge and skill in the art, especially in making mirrors, and their efforts, and those of Germany during both the seventeenth and eighteenth centuries had a most injurious effect on the industry of Murano. The invention and immediate popularity of the colorless Bohemian glass, which resulted in the process of cutting glass—a method of ornamentation for which the Venetian glass, because of its thinness, was ill-suited—resulted in a further decline in Murano glassmaking, which was not corrected until 1848 when Signor Bussolin revived several of the ancient processes of Venetian glassmaking.

The first really new innovation in the art of glassmaking—in regard to content of the materials used—came in 1676 when George Ravenscroft, an Englishman, perfected glass made with a large quantity of lead. The lead glass was softer, heavier, clearer, and more brilliant than the old soda-lime glass.

Glassworkers, at the risk of their lives, had already brought many of the secrets of the Venetian art to almost every country in Europe. Their knowledge, blended with native styles, had produced vigorous new forms. The great eighteenth-century Diderot *Encyclopedie* devoted over one hundred pages to glassmaking in Europe. Illustrations from this volume depict tradi-

Today the use of glass in making objects of art
rivals the craftsmanship of the Renaissance.
"Easter Island" is a fine example from Steuben Glass.

tional techniques employed in eighteenth-century glass-works. With knowledge obtained from the Venetian emigrants and other sources combined with the perfection of Ravenscroft's lead glass (or "flint" glass), the English glassmaking industry flourished. The English developed sturdy, simple forms to show the clearest glass yet made in its best light.

By the middle of the eighteenth century London, Bristol, Birmingham, and Waterford had become important centers of glassmaking and were producing excellent examples of fine bowls and the English glass drinking vessel which became the clean-lined, classic vessel of today, the model for most of the glasses of the modern world.

There was little progress in the development of using or altering raw materials in the manufacture of glass until the late eighteenth century when Pierre Louis Guinand, a Swiss glassmaker, developed a method of stirring glass in the molten state. His technique produced a more homogenous composition: an optical glass with only a few physical imperfections. Guinand's work and subsequent studies in France pointed the way to a complete investigation of the possible constituents of glass. These developments substantially met one of the two basic requirements for production of optical glass: freedom from physical imperfections.

The search for the second requirement—more than one type of glass—began in the early nineteenth century and led to experiments in adding new ingredients to the glass batch. This systematic search in the field of producing new and different glasses, pioneered by a German named Otto Schott, resulted in the introduction of more than twenty-five entirely new elements for use in glassmaking.

The first glassworks established in America was in Jamestown, Virginia, in 1608. However, it soon failed and a successful glassworks was not founded until 1739 when the Wistarberg, New Jersey, works of Caspar Wistar was established. By 1825, when a method of pressing hot glass in a metal mold was perfected, the United States glass industry was firmly established and meeting the competition of foreign imports.

Building on the work of such men as Schott, the glass industry has undergone a revolution in the last century. Liberated from the limiting bonds of a few recipes for the manufacture of glass, and aided by modern machine technology, glassmakers have waged an extensive investigation of glass compositions.

Their work has resulted in tens of thousands of workable glass compositions which use almost every element on the earth's surface. And while the art of the glassmaker has not been abolished—in fact, it has thrived—the versatility of glass has made it a basic engineering material. As a matter of fact, were it not for the modern glass industry, Apollo 11 would not have reached the lunar surface to bring back samples of volcanic glass.

100 YEARS OF COLLEGE FOOTBALL

By Walter Jarrett

*O*ne hundred years ago on the afternoon of November 6, 1869, the first intercollegiate football game took place at New Brunswick, New Jersey, between Princeton and Rutgers. For years a spirited rivalry in sports, debate, and other traditional customs had existed between the two schools and a form of football was already popular at both universities—as well as at several other Eastern schools. For years both Rutgers and Princeton had fielded class teams that played an intermural schedule and in 1867 Princeton had fielded one team made up of the best players from its "class teams" that played several games with the Princeton Seminary.

The fellows at Rutgers felt that the best of their 1869 class teams was better than Princeton's all-school team. William Leggett, a Rutgers student who later be-

183

came a noted clergyman, is credited with the idea of sending the challenge to Princeton to play a series of three football matches, the first to take place on November 6 at New Brunswick, the second at Princeton on November 13, and the third at New Brunswick on November 29. The Princeton team, naturally, accepted the challenge.

There was, of course, no set standard of rules for the game in 1869. Rutgers had been using a set of rules very similar to the English Rugby game, while the Princeton rules were somewhat similar to those used in the game of soccer. It was decided, after some discussion, that the first match would be played by Rutgers rules, such as they were.

Twenty-five men were picked to play on each side, with Rutgers captained by Leggett. William Gummere, who was later to become chief justice of the Supreme Court of New Jersey, was captain of the Princeton team.

Very little is remembered about the first encounter except that a member of the Rutgers faculty, upon noticing that Princeton was considerably larger than the home team, tried to stop the game. Princeton wore no colors but the Rutgers players wore scarlet handkerchiefs tied about their heads, giving birth to the school color.

There was much singing and yelling—as a matter of fact, college yells were born during that first game when a group of Princeton students, who had traveled to New Brunswick to see their team "put the farmers of Rutgers in their place," originated the famed Princeton "sis-boom-bah" yell.

There were two powerful players with Princeton besides Captain Gummere, Mike Michaels and Colonel Weir, a Civil War veteran, but while Princeton was larger and stronger, Rutgers was much better trained and better organized—and were playing by their set of rules. Also it appears that Princeton was, in the first intercollegiate game, a victim of over-confidence—a malady that still contributes to the upsets of strong teams by weaker opponents. Much to Princeton's surprise, Rutgers won the game six goals to four. Before the game it had been decided that the team that scored the first six goals would be the winner.

The second game, as previously scheduled, was played at Princeton on November 13. This time Rutgers agreed to follow the Princeton rules and the team scoring the first eight goals would be declared the victor. Princeton won eight goals to zero.

However, the faculties of both schools decided that the game was not only much too rough but a waste of time, and thus succeeded in cancelling the third game.

The two games played by Princeton and Rutgers in 1869 were the beginning of intercollegiate football, but a form of it had been in existence since ancient times. The Eskimos and various islanders of the South Pacific were playing a form of "football" when first discovered by Europeans. The ancient Greeks played a game that bore a resemblance to the modern one, mentioned in Smith's *Dictionary of Antiquities:* "It was the game of football, played in much the same way as with us, by a great number of persons divided into two parties opposed to one another."

The Romans picked up the sport from the Greeks and called it "harpastum." And while harpastum was a gymnastic game and probably performed indoors, the Romans also played a form of football in the open with an inflated *follis* which was kicked from side to side over boundaries and quite possibly resembled the modern English Rugby, from which American football was to later evolve.

The Roman legions introduced their version of football into Northern Europe and Great Britain, although

The first intercollegiate football game between Rutgers and Princeton, November 6, 1869. Rutgers won 6–4.

Irish antiquarians assert that a variety of football has been played in Ireland for over two thousand years. In early times the great football festival was held on Shrove Tuesday, though the connection of the game with this particular date is lost in obscurity. William Fitzstephen, in his *History of London*, tells of the young men of the twelfth century going into the fields to play the well-known game of football on this day.

Two centuries later the game fell into such disrepute that it was forbidden by Edward II in 1314 in consequence of "the great noise in the city caused by hustling over large balls." Again in 1365 Edward III prohibited the sport "on account of the decadence of archery" as did Richard II, for exactly the same reason, in 1388. Both Henry VIII and Elizabeth I enacted laws against football as being "too violent."

In Stubbes' *Anatomie of Abuses* (1583) football is referred to as "a devilishe pastime . . . and hereof groweth envy, rancour and malice, and sometimes brawling, murther, homicide, and great effusion of blood."

Fifty years later Davenant is quoted in Hone's *Table-Book* as remarking, "I would now make a safe retreat, but me thinks I am stopped by one of your heroic games called football; which I conceive (under your favour) not very conveniently civil in the streets, especially in such irregular and narrow roads as Crooked Lane. Yet it argues your courage, much like your military pastime of throwing at cocks, since you have long allowed these two valiant exercises in the streets."

As evidence of the popularity of the game in Ireland, the statues of Galway in 1527 forbade every other sport save archery, excepting "onely the great foot balle." In the time of Charles II, football was popular at Cambridge, particularly at Magdalene College.

Nevertheless, football remained for the most part a game for the masses and never took root, except in

*Toward the end of the last century football became
so rough that it drew a public outcry.*

The Princeton-Yale game of 1879. The game ended in a tie, spoiling Yale's perfect record.

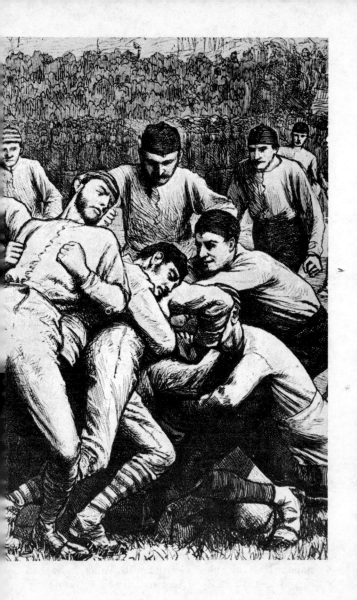

educational institutions, among the upper classes until the nineteenth century. No clubs or code of rules had been formed, and the sole aim seems to have been to drive the ball through the opposing side's goal by means fair or foul.

So rough did the game become that James I forbade the heir apparent to participate and describes the exercise in his *Basilikon Doron* as "meeter for laming than making able the users thereof." Both sexes and all ages seem to have taken part in it on Shrove Tuesday when shutters had to be put up and houses closed in order to prevent damage, and it is quite understandable why the game fell into bad repute. Accidents, sometimes fatal, occurred and Shrove Tuesday, "football day," gradually died out about 1830.

After that date football was practiced only at the great English public schools. Only at Rugby—and later at some other schools—which possessed an extensive grass field on which to play the game, was the old form of football preserved and developed, including even its roughness for actual "hacking" (intentionally kicking an opponent's legs) which was not expressly abolished at Rugby until 1877.

The English form of football was brought to the Colonies by the Pilgrims and, in time, became a part of the Thanksgiving Day festivities. The game was being played at Harvard in the 1820's. An account in the October, 1827, *Harvard Register* mentions the roughness of the sport, "unnumbered bruised shins and coats torn to pieces." Yale and Princeton took up the game about 1840. At all three schools it was played as the general sport among students until the beginning of the War Between the States.

During the Civil War several high schools in the Boston area played football matches but there was no standard set of rules. Gerrit Smith Miller, who had played football at Epes Sargent Dixwell Private Latin

School in Boston, organized the first football club, along with graduates of other Boston high schools, in 1862—the Oneida Football Club of Boston. For three years the club took on all comers and not only went undefeated, but was unscored on, developing a set of rules that later became known as the "Boston Rules."

Following the Princeton-Rutgers games of 1869, Columbia took up the sport in 1870 and played Rutgers (losing three goals to six). Rutgers also played Princeton again in 1870 and lost two goals to six. As the three teams could not agree on a standard set of rules coupled with the objections to the game by the faculties of Princeton, Rutgers, and Columbia, no competitions were played in 1871.

The next year all three schools resumed football and both Yale and Stevens Tech fielded teams. That year Columbia attempted the first field goal against Rutgers. New York University took up the game in 1873 and Harvard fielded its first team in 1874 as did McGill and Tufts. The first Harvard team improvised a uniform of magenta and white sweaters and magenta-colored handkerchiefs bound around their heads. By 1879 Wesleyan, Pennsylvania, Amherst, Brown, Michigan, Centre, and Kentucky were fielding football teams. Centre and Kentucky played each other twice in 1879 (Kentucky won both times) but after that initial year both teams dropped football. Centre resumed play in 1891 and Kentucky took up the game in 1892.

The early college football game was a most primitive affair and it wasn't until 1905, when there were 18 deaths and 149 serious injuries reported for the season, that Walter Camp, the "father of college football," called an intercollegiate meeting (after President Theodore Roosevelt issued an angry ultimatum to clean up college football or he would ban it by Presidential edict) to revamp the rules and make the game safer, that the rules became uniform and the game began to

LUMBIA TOPS ARMY, 21-20,
ENN DOWNS NAVY, 21-0; C

As Unbeaten Army Finally Bowed

Kusserow of the Lions maneuvering to get away a pass in the second quarter of the game.

HIT HARD

Power to Score
Last Quarter
nst Navy

LONG MARCHES

5 and 50 Yards
205 Spectators
anklin Field

Stymie Triumphs to Regain
World Money-Winning Lead

MICHIGAN TOPPL
MINNESOTA 13

---

*By 1947 college football had become an American
institution as can be seen by this sports page from*
The New York Times.

DING CADET STREAK AT 32
NELL AND DARTMOUTH W.

mbia at Baker Field Yesterday

LIONS SCORE L

Army Has 20-7 L
Half-Time, but
to Columbia R

AERIALS SINK THE

Swiacki: Brilliant as Re
Yablonski's Kick De
Kusserow Counts

By LOUIS EFF
Columbia 21, Army 20

his teammates Rossides (2) and Swiacki, who is blocking Kellom (85) of the Cadets

nell's Rally Subdues
Princeton by 28 to 21

DARTMOUTH STOPS
HARVARD 14 TO 13

resemble today's college football.

The eastern colleges lost their stranglehold on the National Football Championship in 1902 when Michigan went undefeated for the second year in a row (after starting the year off with a 49-0 defeat of Stanford in the Rose Bowl) and tied Yale for the National Championship. The aerial game became respectable after an unheralded Notre Dame tea mused it to upset a strong Army team in 1913. As gridiron power began to spread across the country, the college game became wilder yearly as such teams as Georgia Tech, Sewanee, Vanderbilt, Centre, Carlisle, Chicago, and Washington State became powerhouses.

Particularly in the years between 1910 and 1920 college teams vied with each other in running up seemingly impossible scores (although Yale had started it all back in 1884 by defeating Dartmouth 113-0). The Georgia Tech team of 1916 showed no mercy in defeating Cumberland 222-0 only a week after Cumberland had lost to Sewanee 107-0. That same year St. Viator whipped Lane 205-0, Rice slaughtered Southern Methodist 146-3, Oklahoma beat Shawnee Catholic 140-0, Ohio State topped Oberlin 128-0, Tulsa beat Missouri Mines 117-0, Morningside whipped Nebraska 116-0 and just to prove it wasn't a fluke, defeated Dakota Wesleyan by the same score later in the season.

The oldest organized college football conference was formed in 1893 as the Southern Intercollegiate Athletic Association and consisted of approximately thirty teams. The conference was reorganized in 1922 and consisted of twenty teams scattered from Maryland to Louisiana. Finally the conference was split in 1932 to form the Southern and Southeastern conferences.

The Big Ten, originally known as the Western Conference, was formed in 1895 and consisted of Chicago, Illinois, Michigan, Minnesota, Wisconsin, Northwestern, and Purdue. The Missouri Valley Conference was formed in 1907 but split in 1927 to form the Big Eight and the Missouri Valley conferences. The Southwest Conference was formed in 1914. The beginnings of Rocky Mountain Conference are obscure, as are those of the Ivy League which was not formally organized until recent times (although both were declaring a "Conference Champion" by 1900). The Pacific Coast Intercollegiate A.A. was formed in 1915 but was reorganized in the 1950's. Both Idaho and Montana were formerly members of the Pacific Coast.

From its obscure beginnings at New Brunswick, New Jersey, in 1869, American College football has evolved into the present-day game—a game that, with the aid of television, often draws fifty million spectators on a Saturday afternoon—as compared with the three hundred who watched the first game!

*The first Lord MacDonald and his brother,
Sir James, playing golf*

A HISTORY OF GOLF

by Rudolph Brasch

No one knows for certain how golf began. Most scholars assume that the name came from the German or Dutch word for club, *kolbe* or *kolf*, and that some form of the game was played in prehistoric times with a branch and a pebble. Hitting stones with a stick seems to be instinctive and that, it is thought, is what shepherds did in the pre-Christian era. Sir W. G. Simpson explained the beginnings of golf in Scotland in that way. In a story, he told of sheep on a stretch of ground that was to become part of the St. Andrews golf links in Fifeshire. To pass the time, the shepherd knocked pebbles about with his crook, until one fell by chance into a rabbit hole. When he tried to repeat the shot, a friend who was watching challenged him; the first golf match in the land of the heather resulted, each player trying to sink his pebble in the rabbit hole.

It is a historical fact that a sport popular among the ancient Romans. known as *paganica,* was a forerunner of modern golf. This "game of the countrymen" was played with a bent stick and a leather ball stuffed with feathers. As Roman legions marched across Europe, it is most likely they carried the game with them and it was adopted by the conquered nation. There are many other suggestions about the introduction of golf to Scotland. Similarities to hurley, or shinty, led people to trace the game to the ancient Celtic equivalent of English hockey. Supporting their claim, they quoted an Ulster legend in which one of its heroes, Cuchullain, set out on a journey taking with him his hurley and silver ball. To speed himself up he gave the ball a stroke with the hurley, driving it a great distance ahead. He continued to do so throughout the journey.

Most frequently, the Dutch have been credited with being the fathers of golf. Their game of *kolven* certainly had some of golf's features. It was played either on the ice of frozen lakes or canals, or on a court. This latter was mostly paved and known as the *kolf bann.* Contestants tried to hit, with a minimum of strokes, two sticks placed at opposite ends of the court. However, the ball used was the size of a grapefruit and weighed two pounds, and the many paintings (among them an etching by Rembrandt) on which the claim is based stem from a time at least two hundred years after golf had definitely been established in Scotland. Yet another theory sees in golf an adaptation of the Flemish game of *chole,* known to have been played as early as 1353. This was a cross-country pursuit, in which both sides played the same ball with a mallet, taking turns to make three strokes each. The goal sometimes as far as a mile away, was some conspicuous landmark, such as a tree or a gateway.

Though all these games resembled golf in some ways,

they obviously were not exactly like it. Golf is unique and, no doubt, the result of a natural evolution of some of these early sports. Records show that a kind of golf was played in Scotland during the 15th century, and it has been pointed out many times that the game reveals characteristics in keeping with the Scots' reserve, caution and meticulous care. Only a Scot, it has been contended, could have created a contest that combined such features as hitting a small ball across rough country to a hole in the ground, without his opponent having the right to interfere in any way.

The earliest existing reference to the game talks more against it than about it. Authorities regarded it most unfavorably and did not hesitate to express objections to it. In 1457, the Scottish Parliament voiced the opinion that playing golf was gravely interfering with more important pursuits of archery and ordained that golf be "utterly cryit doun, and nocht usit." At the time, people lived in constant fear of invasion. Bows and arrows were instruments of war, and every male citizen was compelled to practise archery daily to perfect his markmanship. But when instead of training for their country's defense men wasted their time in hitting small balls for their own pleasure, the government had to step in and declare the game illegal.

Apparently such prohibitions were only for a limited period. At all events golf became increasingly popular and, eventually, royalty not only gave the sport their blessing but began to enjoy it themselves. Records of the lord treasurer for 1503-6 show use of the crown's money for golf balls. Both Charles I and James II loved the game. Mary, Queen of Scots, was the first woman golfer. She played several rounds only a few days after the murder of her husband. And during her reign (about 1552) St. Andrews of Scotland was established —the most famous of all golf courses. No wonder that the Scotsman could speak of "the Royal and Ancient

Game of Golf."

Inevitably the game spread, and the first golf societies were formed in England in the eighteenth century. These made use of public land, meeting at inns before and after their rounds. The world's first golf tournament took place in 1860 at Prestwick, Scotland. The winner received a belt for his trophy and permanent property. The first rules intended to be adopted universally were laid down, as was only to be expected, by St. Andrews in 1882.

Possibly Scottish regiments (but definitely Scottish emigrants) first took the game to America where it was played occasionally during the Revolutionary War. However, John G. Reid, of Yonkers, New York, has been called "the father of American golf." During the 1880's he interested a group of friends in the game, and America's first golf club, St. Andrews, resulted from their activities.

Golf actually means a club. At first they were improvised cudgels cut from a tree or a hedgerow and made of a single piece of wood. These sticks were bent or curved at the striking end which sometimes was studded with flints. Such clubs were crude and clumsy, and it did not take long for their many disadvantages to become apparent. The need for improvement urged on man's inventive spirit, and step followed step in the creation of our modern clubs.

The first and most significant advance (not later than the 15th century) was the introduction of separate heads. Still made of wood, mostly of oak branches, the original length was extended to six inches. Their height was one inch and their depth one and one-fourth inch. They had little loft and were joined to the blackthorn shaft by splicing and binding. Gradually the heads became smaller, and the first truly lofted clubs came into existence. They were known as spoons or baffies. The next stage in the club's evolution was the replacement of a wooden head with an iron one. This was attached to a shaft made of hickory. The first iron heads were extremely heavy and thick with a short face. Once again, experience led the way, and soon a great variety of clubs was produced, each having a different degree of loft with the heads much lighter and the hitting surfaces larger.

A shortage of hickory wood and an ever growing public demand for golf equipment created new problems. Manufacturers experimented with other materials, such as bamboo and steel. In the 1920's, American golfers chose tubular steel for their shafts instead of hickory. At first this shaft was outlawed, as it was felt it would increase greatly the distance of a drive thereby necessitating expensive lengthening of most courses. However, in 1926, the new club was officially accepted. There was an ample supply of steel and, using it, the sticks were produced much more quickly and in greater numbers. The new type of club soon became so popular that, in spite of initial objections from Scotland's conservative St. Andrews which considered the introduction of the steel shaft "detrimental to the professional trade in the country," within 10 years it was adopted all over the world.

At first clubs were carried loosely under the arm. The introduction of the golf bag goes back to the 1870's and the thoughtfulness of a retired sailmaker employed as a clubhouse attendant at the famous links of the Royal North Devon Club at Westard Ho!, England. Still endowed with memories of his former trade and, no doubt, also with some of its raw materials, he thought (most probably on a rainy day) a strip of canvas would keep the sticks' grips dry. From his protective covering the modern bag evolved.

But golf's most important accouterment is the ball. So small in itself, the number of rules that govern its treatment by far exceeds those relating to any other feature of the game. The ball's dimension has even drawn a dividing line between English-speaking people; its American girth is slightly, though noticeably, larger than that of its British brother. The official English ball measures 1.62 inches in diameter and the American, 1.68 inches.

Keeping our eye on the history of the ball we can follow an interesting development. There is no doubt that, like in kindred sports of those days, at an early date balls were made of turned boxwood. This is confirmed by a document of 1363 which describes a game of "a crooked stick or curved club or playing mallet with which a small wooden ball was propelled forward." However, the most popular ball then, like its Roman prototype, was made of feathers. Its production demanded much care and time.

Small thin segments of leather, usually three pieces of untanned cowhide, were stitched together to form a bag. The opening which was left served a twofold purpose. First, it was used to turn the ball inside out so the stitches would be on the inside. Then sufficient feathers were boiled to fill a top hat and, by means of a pike, stuffed tightly through the hole into the bag. This done, the hole was sewn up and the ball hand rubbed with white paint. Meanwhile, the feathers, in drying, expanded and gave the ball extra resilience. Obviously its quality and liveliness much depended upon how tightly the feathers had been packed. Altogether, making a ball was a job for experts, and those early handmade missiles were greatly treasured and highly priced.

It was soon realized that the *featherie*, as the ball was called, was inadequate. In rainy weather it quickly became sodden and heavy. It seldom stayed round, and when scuffed with an iron frequently split open. Worst of all, it would not travel any great distance. Players began to experiment with other types, aiming at finding a ball that was weatherproof, more nearly round and, not least, cheaper. Success came in 1848. A solid ball was moulded from coagulated juice of the gutta-percha tree. This substance was then mostly used for the insulation of submarine cables. At first this *guttie* was smooth as a billiard ball but later showed several faults. Its flight was erratic, and after it had traveled some distance it dropped like a dead bird. No wonder that the featherie makers, feeling their livelihood threatened, took hold of such incidents to ridicule the novel ball and point out that after all their product was still much superior.

But they did not laugh for long. A professional player became disappointed enough with the new balls that he gave them to his caddy. One day, watching him at play, he was more than surprised to note the balls, although by then battered, could be hit much more efficiently than his own featheries. It seemed that the more hacked the gutties were the better they flew. The fact was the dents and cuts, either from the club or the impact of stones and trees, improved the guttie's flying power by offering sufficient resistance to the air to give the missile a more consistent trajectory.

Damaged balls, so to speak, were thus at a premium. But why wait for a ball to become battered to be able to play a good game? Would it not be far easier to produce a ball without a smooth surface by artificially notching it? Such a ball was made, a guttie systematically nicked by hand. It was the birth of the modern pattern of our golf ball. Eventually, in 1880, someone got the idea of streamlining the whole process, and instead of hand-hammering each individual ball, began to put the many markings on its surface by means of a pock-marked mould. Another fault of the early guttie was its habit of breaking up after rough handling. But even this was not a loss. The various pieces easily could be melted down and remoulded into a completely new ball.

The invention of the guttie revolutionized the game. Whereas the featherie was costly and took a long time to make, the new ball could be fabricated cheaply in vast quantities. Golf was thereby no longer restricted to the wealthy classes. Until the coming of the guttie no definite rules existed about the weight and size of the ball. The new manufacturing process changed that as well and led to the standardization of the ball's measurements. Gutties were used until the turn of the century, when the rubber-core ball, invented by Americans, replaced it.

There are still doubts about the original meaning of "putt." Some suggest that the word is derived from the Dutch *putten*, meaning "to place in a hole." However, Robert H. K. Browning relates the term to the Highland sport of "putting the weight" and asserts that the putt once described any shot that started a ball off on a low trajectory.

Equal controversy concerns the first tee, which has been traced to both Gaelic and Dutch. The Gaelic word *tigh* literally meant "a house." But in sport it referred to the marked spot on which players of the ancient Scottish game of curling tried to hurl large rounded stones. The Dutch *tuitse* (pronounced toytee), on the other hand, was the little mound of sand from which Dutchmen used to shoot the ball. And which, in fact, was the earliest, earth-made tee.

Originally, the teeing ground was very small and situated within a club length of the hole. Indeed, players often shaped their tees from sand which they took from the hole itself. Actually, tee-pegs were preceded by all kinds of props, including beer bottles. The general rules still adhered to merely demand "the ball may be placed on the ground or on sand or other substance to raise it off the gound." It was a much later development that divided putting greens from the teeing ground which, as a separate entity, was mentioned for the first time in 1875.

At first, holes had no standard measure. Their diameter of four and one-half inches was introduced quite by chance. Two golfers on St. Andrews found that one hole was so badly worn they could not use it. Much of its sand had been removed by previous players for building tees. Anxious to repair the damage and continue their game, they looked around and discovered nearby part of an old drain pipe. They inserted this in the hole. It was the first cup, and because it happened to measure four and one-half inches across, all cups are now that size.

Much care is now given to laying out and keeping up golf courses. During the earliest periods of the game the players chose the most suitable grass-covered stretches of land, which were called links. This explains the application of that term for a golf course ever since.

Gullies and shrubs were the earliest hazards, and nature itself looked after the course. Rabbits cropped the grass, birds' droppings fertilized the ground whilst sheep and other stray animals contributed their part in manure as well as in the creation of bunkers. The course the players followed was not predetermined but selected each time rather haphazardly. There were no fixed tees. Golfers simply picked the most convenient clear patch from which to drive the ball toward one of five or six holes. With the development of the game these became more numerous. Sometimes there were as many as twenty holes.

Even the present traditional number of eighteen holes is completely accidental and certainly not the result of a deliberate choice. It merely shows the power of fashion and man's imitative urge. Originally there were no hard and fast rules on the number of holes golfers had to play. They ranged between five and twenty. The Honorable Company of Edinburgh Golfers, established in 1744, was soon regarded the top club, and

Blackheath, 1876

anything it chose to do set a fashion. All clubs were proud when they could point out that they were following Edinburgh's examples. At first its course had a mere five holes and was between four and five hundred yards long. The official round then consisted of playing the holes three times, fifteen holes all told.

When the links at Blackheat were laid out, it was not surprising that they adopted the identical number and kind of play. But, significantly, as soon as Edinburgh extended its course to seven holes, almost automatically Blackheat followed suit. And had Edinburgh preserved its leading place in the world of golf, probably no one would ever have dreamt of eighteen holes. And yet a mere name, however famous, is not sufficient to retain leadership. Because Edinburgh's links were not the best, slowly but surely St. Andrews took over leadership and eventually clubs everywhere based their rules on those of St. Andrews.

Originally St. Andrews had twelve holes. The golfer started his game by teeing up next to the home hole. He then played eleven holes which led him to the far end of the course. Turning back he played the holes again in the reverse direction. Hence the total number of holes played was twenty-two. In 1764, it was decided to convert the first four holes into two, reducing the total to eighteen. What had been done at St. Andrews was soon noted, and the playing of eighteen holes became the fashion and later the standard. The actual number of holes was still only nine. Much later St. Andrews realized that playing twice over nine holes for a round of eighteen was far from satisfactory and introduced separate fairways and greens for the outward and homeward journeys.

Bunkers, too, came into existence accidentally. They were the result of wear and tear assisted by the forces of nature. The old-fashioned lifting irons soon ruined turf and the continuous trampling by players caused

William Gunn at Bruntsfield Links, near Edinburgh.
From an 1839 painting

bald patches. The wind blew away the light soil and created a sandy hollow. This process was especially noticeable on courses near the sea. Players tried to confine the hollow with railway sleepers and other timber to which they nailed planks for shoring.

Contestants quickly discovered that the damaged parts of the course made the game more exciting by adding new challenges. The bunker, though proving a trap to the unwary, was a boon to the skillful. Clubs with courses laid out on firmer ground and away from the windswept dune country along the sea began to imitate the bunker and to create it artificially. They were adopted by Tom Dunn, pioneer of golf architecture, and became so popular that ever since they have been a standard feature of every course.

That the caddy has traveled a long distance is not surprising. In his case there is no doubt of ancestry though. Typically enough, he has fallen very much from his aristocratic beginnings. His home was France, where at the time he was far removed from games and golf. The word caddy is derived from the French *cadet*, meaning "a little chief," a title mostly used for the younger sons of nobility. Mary, Queen of Scots, introduced it into Scotland where it was soon sarcastically applied to any type of hanger-on. In fact the noble word deteriorated so much that in Edinburgh it was bestowed on messengers, errand boys and porters waiting for an odd job.

Caddy then described any kind of porter and only later specifically referred to the porter who carried golf sticks. It was also his job to clean them with emery paper during and after the game. Still carrying on the porter's French pronunciation, cad-day, the British began to spell it their own way, and that is how cadet changed into caddy.

Later his task extended far beyond transportation and cleaning of clubs. Before the introduction of tee-pegs, making tees belonged to his duties as well. He did so mostly by taking a handful of sand out of the hole or the tee-box (which has also deteriorated in value and changed into the present day refuse receptable) and putting it onto the turf, shaping it into a small cone on top of which (like into a volcano's crater) he placed the ball.

Links originally were not reserved for golfers. They also served other purposes such as horse racing, cricket, children's games, grazing for cows and sheep, drying of fishermen's nets and laundry which housewives had washed in nearby creeks or the sea. A golfer needed a guide to avoid those many obstacles, and at first it was the caddy's job to lead the way and find the hole, which he marked with a gull's feather or a broken-off branch, the forerunner of the modern flag stick. Indeed, caddies developed an elaborate code of signals to indicate to their employers the best course to follow. Eventually, the caddy became an expert advisor, who told his master not only which way to go, but which club to use. Perhaps he, most of all, learned to appreciate the finer points of the game of golf and was its best critic and most ardent enthusiast.

John Barrymore in Don Juán

THE SYNCHRO-NIZATION OF DON JUAN

By Whitney Stine

*F*orty years ago the screen was learning to talk. The parents of this rather squeaky phenomenon were four men, the Warner brothers. The grandfathers were Thomas A. Edison and Alexander Graham Bell; its uncles were a handful of scared technicians. The birth was carried out in secrecy without even a midwife in attendance, and the baby was actually torn from its electrical womb by men who half expected it to be stillborn.

Today, four decades later, silent movies to half the population mean Charlie Chaplin, Buster Keaton and a few other shadows who dart with great alacrity over the TV screen on a Saturday morning children's show. By and large, younger folk have grown up regularly attending movies with talking and laughing and singing, amplified by four tracks of sterophonic sound, elongated into Cinemascope or enlarged to 70mm. To them sound film is like Winnie The Pooh—it always was.

In 1925, the Warner brothers, Albert, Harry, Sam and Jack, held forth from a small studio on Sunset Boulevard in Hollywood. They made prestige films with such stars as John Barrymore, Marie Prevost, Monte Blue and Fannie Brice, but the star who was the least tempermental and who brought in the most money was a dog—Rin Tin Tin. He had kept the wolf from the door for many years. The studio was suffering the pains of over-expansion brought on by the acquiring of its present location, the purchase of another studio, Vitagraph in New York, the building up of a chain of theatres to show its films, and expensive pictures that did not bring back expected returns. The Warner Brothers were on the brink of disaster.

The timing could not have been more opportune or unexpected. Fate in this case was an engineer. Benjamin Levinson, who worked for Western Electric Company, had become friendly with the most sympathetic of the brothers, Sam, who himself had picked up a little technical knowledge by working on bicycles as a boy and a little later by projecting films in a tent show. Levinson's aims were not altogether altruistic. A cohort, Walter J. Rich, a kind of promoter who had collaborated with Western Electric to interest Hollywood in synchronized pictures, failed miserably when he tried to interest the major studios in this new device. Rich had been politely, but firmly, shown out of the front live-voice trailer. The list of disasters connected with sound was long, complicated and unrewarding.

The big studios were not interested in sound. Countless reputations and considerable fortunes had been thrown by the wayside in experiments with the novelty. Dr. Lee DeForest's glowlight process was actually "booed" at a preview in New York, and Norma Shearer's brother, Douglas, was once fired by M.G.M. for publicizing one of his sister's films with a film-and-live-voice trailer. The list of disasters connected with sound was long, complicated and unrewarding.

Sam Warner, however, was less skeptical than Levinson expected and accepted an invitation to the Bell Laboratories in New York. The films that were projected that memorable day were no more than bits of disjointed celluloid with such noisy accompaniment that what was meant to be heard was almost drowned out by scratchy surface racket. Sam was not very imaginative in an artistic sense, but he had a tinker's brain. He was suddenly filled with a vision of what this apparatus could mean to an audience. He knew very well that silent films, no matter how artfully cut together and subtly titled, were at their best a kind of turbulent battleground through which the spectator had to fight his way. But, with this synchronization, this marvelous force which drew words and music from the very mouths of the performers, the audience, formerly only spectators, became active participants in what was taking place on the screen. They became involved at once. There was no warm-up period to get accustomed to the mood of the picture. Sam fell in love with this talking, this singing, this music, this mixing of image with sound.

Two processes were shown that day. The first was disc-and-film, but in the second the sound was recorded directly on the edge of the film. In the first method, the disc was recorded at the same time as the picture was shot, then played back simultaneously. In the second device, by the use of a sound head on the projector, a little light shined through the sound track and reverted the dialogue, which had been turned into electronic impulses, back into sound. Sam preferred the disc method which took the phonograph one step further, into the projection room, and he promised Levinson he would try to interest his brothers but he did not hold much hope.

Sam went back to Hollywood with a heavy heart. He believed in disc-and-film, but he also knew the problems at the studio and the grey days that his brothers faced financially. How could he approach them with a hare-brained scheme that could possibly cost thousands of dollars at a time when it was even difficult to meet payroll? Still, it was worth a chance. But, Harry, fraught with finance, Albert, distraught with distribution, and Jack, puzzled with pictures, would not hear him out. Sam bided his time. A few weeks later, Sam and Levinson invited the brothers over to Bell Laboratories on the ruse of a social get-together, ushered them into the projection room, turned out the lights and presented the experimental films.

The first short was a stutterer, the second, a singer and the third, a small orchestra. The lights came up, Harry stood up and addressed Levinson. "The music was first rate. Dialogue, you can live without, but music may be the answer! By using this device to accompany silent pictures, you open a new world. It's good to hear, and the exhibitor can save a lot of money by eliminating the piano player or the organist. They can buy the whole package in one operation. Talking pictures themselves are not even a possibility, but this use of music, I can see." It was common knowledge that exhibitors recently had had to bring everything into their theatres from live prologues and vaudeville to full orchestras to entice the public inside. Something was wrong with the movie business, but no one knew what it was.

Now that the Warners had furtively decided to go along on the sound experiments, Harry called Walter J. Rich and it was proposed that they go fifty-fifty on the deal, with the studio putting in $72,000 to the $36,000 that Rich had already invested. Harry then unwisely told Western Electric that he was going to use the film-and-disc device to accompany silent pictures.

Western Electric officials, impressed solely with the spoken word, greeted his news with misgivings because they had not considered synchronized musical scores. Already they began to regret they had signed the deal with such a small outfit.

Although the Warners tried to carry on the sound experiments in secrecy, word got out about what was going on at Bell Laboratories. Instead of big film producers being worried, they laughed contemptuously. What were the Warners trying to pull off? Hadn't they heard about DeForest and Shearer and all the other would-be miracle workers? Why should the Warner/Bell endeavor turn out differently.

Sam audited the engineering experiments with an eye to the technical end. The big question was how to synchronize the film-to-disc process. Silent films were photographed with speeds usually running around 16 frames per second. Hollywood producers furnished cue sheets for projectionists, who could then (by manipulating the rheostat) change the speed of the machine to correspond with the action on the screen. With sound films, a corresponding film speed that would be the same all the time and still match the 33⅓ revolutions per minute of the disc turntable had to be found because sound had to be recorded and reproduced at the same speed. Finally, after much trial and not a little error, it was discovered that if the projector was set to run 24 frames a second, which was the same speed at which the film was photographed, then perfect synchronization was achieved.

The disc turntable had to be re-designed to fit under the projector where it would be within easy reach of the operators and yet out of the general traffic of the projection booth. Elaborate cue marks were placed on the start of the film, and a wide circle was affixed leading into the first recorded sound on the disc (which was recorded on the disc from the inside out). By carefully aligning these indicators, the timing was perfect, and film matched disc.

While Sam and the engineers worked around the clock to pull together the sound components and perfect the plan for necessary patents, work was stepped up at the studio on the filming of *Don Juan*, which had been selected to be the first motion picture to be released with a musical score. On April 20, 1926, Western Electric licensed Warner Brothers to produce synchronized pictures under its patents. After four hundred names had been discarded, "Vita" was borrowed from Vitagraph, and "phone" from the electrical system between disc and speaker, and the process was christened *Vitaphone*.

Harry, full of plans on exploitation, came out from New York and, after seeing a rough cut of *Don Juan*, told Jack to throw another $200,000 into new scenes involving hundreds of extras and an elaborate chase to be shot at Chatsworth. Barrymore, he felt, had never been more handsome or had a better screen part, and Mary Astor and Estelle Taylor had never been more beautiful.

The Warners knew that they could not get an immediate box office return on *Don Juan*, because there was only one theatre in the world that was equipped to show synchronized film, the Warner Theatre at 52nd Street and Broadway in Manhattan. Hundreds upon hundreds of theatres would have to be wired for sound before money would come in to make up the giant losses already incurred. Harry felt the studio might as well go bankrupt for a few hundred thousand dollars more.

The Warners had to be as ingenious as possible about this first presentation. What the evening needed was class. Several cultural short subjects might be the answer. Sam knew that the Victor Talking Machine Company (not yet purchased by RCA) had many Metropolitan Opera stars under contract, so why not ask a few of these personalities to make their Vitaphone debut? Then the program would automatically have class as well as prestige. He contacted the Victor people and told them of his plan. Money made the difference, borrowed money.

The upshot was that the Warners signed an agreement to pay $52,000 a year to Victor for the stars' release, $24,000 to Brunswick-Balke-Collender Company for the artists under contract, and $104,000 a year for copyrighted music from Composers and Publishers Association. It was a dear price indeed, and some said a foolhardy undertaking, but Alma Gluck, Efrem Zimbalist, Sr., Anna Case, Mischa Elman, Harold Bauer, Giovanni Martinelli, Marion Talley, and others thought differently and were hired on the spot.

On the first day of recording at Vitagraph Studios in Brooklyn, Stanley Watkins (Edison's old assistant from Bell Laboratories) brought along engineers H. C. Humphrey, R. C. Sawyer and George Grove with Ed DuPar, a cameraman, Bert Frank, a cutter, and Herman Heller, the director of the Warner Theatre orchestra in New York. Heller was to direct the first shorts because he was the only one around connected remotely with Warners who knew music. The first day went badly. The stars were in fine voice, the orchestra in excellent shape, the technicians in assured readiness, and even the settings were freshly painted. Martinelli, dressed as a clown, sang *Vesta la Giubba* from *Pagliacci* so movingly even the stagehands were touched.

The record was played back to astonished silence. Martinelli's voice could be heard only dimly in the background of an accumulation of noice: chug, chug, ringing of a bell, strange rustling, patter of feet and, above all, an overtone of hissing that sounded exactly as if a dozen alley cats had formed an impromptu chorus. With difficulty and frayed nerves, each sound was classified separately. The chug, chug was the BMT subway which ran just outside the glassed-in studio; the ringing bell was from the ice cream vendor next door; the rustling was caused by Martinelli's stuffy starched costume, the foot patter by the workmen's shoes. But no one could isolate the dreadful hissing and there was not one pussycat in the entire studio.

Huge signs reading SILENCE were tacked up everywhere, costumes were rented that did not rustle, workmen removed their shoes, a man was hired to time recording sessions between subway schedules, and Watkins himself brought in bolts of monks cloth and acoustically treated the stage. Martinelli began again; again the stagehands wept. The trial disc was rushed back. This time Martinelli and the orchestra shared the disc, as companions in sound, with the chorus of hisses. Where was this maddening unwanted noise originating?

Fearing the building was, indeed, haunted, the Vitaphone Corporation leased the unused Manhattan Opera House, which was promptly turned into the world's first sound stage. The orchestra pit was boarded over to extend the stage. John McCormack's, Louisa Tetrazzini's, and Mary Garden's dressing rooms were turned into, respectively, a recording booth, a workshop, and housing for a group of three-phase alternating current generators. There was not room, however, for the important monitoring apparatus, which ended up on the sixth floor in a room used by a Masonic group. Every time the Masons had a meeting, the equipment was moved out into the hall. Scaffolding was placed over the auditorium seats and arc lights strung from catwalks in the stage loft. Martinelli, again in makeup and costume, faced the camera and the microphone. All was ready. Signals were given, switches thrown, and the famous tones of the Italian tenor floated angelically over the huge house. While the stagehands yawned, the monitors on the sixth floor listened to their head-pieces, hardly daring to breathe.

The disc came back with the hissing intact, as strong or stronger than before! Had the ghost followed Warners all the way over from Brooklyn? Sam thought not, and while the men on the sixth floor developed housemaid knee from running up and down stairs, he put in a emergency call to Warner Brothers' chief electrician Frank Murphy in Hollywood.

In due time the fiery Irishman arrived. He had never been inside an opera house, but he walked all over that stage as if he had always carried a spear. Silently, as he traipsed, his head bobbed up and down like an animal scenting the wind. He drew a long breath and addressed Sam Warner, "It's the lights!"

"It's those hard arcs up there," the little man pointed to the catwalk. "The mike is picking up their sizzle and they are probably giving radio beams off as well." Sam knew that if the engineers were not careful where they set up their dials in connection with recording, radio signals could be picked up from nearby stations. "What are you going to do, Murph?" asked Sam. "Make a new lighting system, using incandescent lamps instead of arcs!" Thus Murphy embarked on an experiment that was to revolutionize the lighting of the motion picture world and be copied by every studio in Hollywood.

The print of *Don Juan* was cut into short scenes and Henry Hadley and his 107-piece orchestra recorded a score by Dr. William Axt and David Mendoza, who took turns timing the scenes with stop watches. Near the opera house, excavation was under way for the Eighth Avenue subway, and adding to the woes of getting the music speeded up or slowed down for certain scenes was a series of dynamite blasts. Hundreds of discs were ruined and hundreds of tempers were lost before the recordings were completed and shipped to the coast.

While the labs were making prints of the film, and the processing plant in San Francisco (Los Angeles had no record plant) was turning out discs, the subject of the premiere came up again. Aside from the operatic shorts and *Don Juan*, Harry and Sam realized that something else was needed, something that would be the capstone of the evening. Sam called Will Hayes, movie censorship head and former postmaster general under Harding's administration, and inquired if he would say a few words before a camera, a kind of introduction to the film. Hayes showed up with a 325-word speech. He, of course, had never been inside a sound stage before and was aghast at all the extra paraphernalia. Afraid that his memory would go on the blink in all the confusion, he asked an assistant to print out the words of his speech on large placards which would be placed outside of camera range. Unbeknownst to him, Will Hayes had created the "idiot card" still popular today on live television.

On the premiere night of August 6, 1926, a line of limousines made their way up Broadway to 52nd Street. John Barrymore's name was in lights the same size as the picture and the magic name of *Vitaphone*. Huge crowds gathered and there was all the excitement of a three-ring circus. But the Warner Brothers were grey with apprehension. At eight-thirty, a hush fell over the audience; two minutes later the house lights dimmed, and the heavy plush curtains parted. Upstairs in the projection room, a carefully rehearsed technician ignited the arc lamps; the sync marks on the film were aligned to those on the disc below; the projector was switched on; and the image of Will Hayes was thrown on the screen a hundred feet below.

The spectators immediately became participants, just as Sam had predicted, en masse. The audience leaned forward to hear what the censorship czar had to say. *He was talking, personally and privately to every one of them!* Hayes eulogized Warners for bringing sound to the screen, and his closing words were: "Now neither the artist nor his act will ever die . . ." Applause rocked the theatre. The collective hearts of the brothers began to beat with a steadier rhythm. Henry Hadley's Overture (to *Tannhauser*) and the Vitaphone shorts brought fresh bursts of applause, then came *Don Juan* with a beautifully timed score that added drama to every sequence.

Harry and Sam felt uneasy, looking at the infrequent titles, but if the picture was good, the music was thrilling. Gradually, tensions ebbed. The stars, some of the best that Hollywood had to offer, swept the film along to the final musically choreographed climax of swordplay and the fade-out kiss of Barrymore and Astor under a painted ersatz moon.

The enthusiasm of the crowd was enormous. Tired happy smiles were glued to the four Warner faces. Everyone, professional and amateur alike, rushed up to compliment anyone who had anything to do with the film. The critics the next morning were unanimous in their praises. New York was overwhelmed. *Don Juan* was only the beginning, ahead lay the 100% talking picture and theatres throughout America proudly proclaimed: THIS THEATRE WIRED FOR SOUND. A playful recipe that ERPI's H. G. Knox gave in 1930, might have been dedicated to those original four men who started it all:

"Take the . . . horn of a radio, the needle of a phonograph, and some studio dust, moistened with the tears of a producer, and make a record. The record is cremated in an electrical laboratory, the ashes wrapped in a film of celluloid and placed on the doorstep of the Motion Picture Industry . . ."

Vladimir K. Zworykin patented his
Iconoscope camera tube in 1925.

EARLY TELEVISION: KINGDOM OF SHADOWS

By Whitney Stine

ormer Federal Communications Commission head, Newton Minnow, called the television industry a "vast wasteland," and writer and raconteur, Goodman Ace, cracked that "TV is called a medium because it is rarely well done." But to Dr. Norman Vincent Peale, who is "an average TV viewer," the greatest thing about the medium is that you can tune in what you do like and tune out what you don't like. Comedian Mort Sahl deplores the comedy/variety shows that are ". . . forced by the limit of good taste to warm up the audience with outhouse humor and then go on the air singing hymns."

One of the most celebrated lines in the 1950 Oscar winning film, *All About Eve,* wryly concerned Marilyn Monroe, who inquired of George Sanders if television was next after failing a stage audition. "Audition?"

Sanders replied laconically, "That's all television is, my dear." But the "glory box" can even laugh at itself, as when the pixyish Henry Gibson on "Laugh-In" twangs plaintively, "Marshall McLuhan, what're 'a doin'?" about the self-styled communications expert whose books and articles microscopically explore the electronic demon.

But *television*—meaning literally "seeing at a distance"—has actually been possible since the last half of the nineteenth century. Its perfection as a communications medium, however, was delayed for several reasons, some strictly scientific and others decidedly human. The technical discovery of one man would lay dormant for years waiting for the next man to take up the cudgel of progress. Each phase of what we now know as television was developed separately. Eight wars, several intra-country disputes, various civil outbreaks, and a couple of revolutions delayed television research some fifty years. Otherwise, with radio becoming a minor craze as early as 1910, the world would have probably had a workable audio-video system by 1914!

The fathers of television were inventors, chemists, telegraphers, scientists, physicists, and engineers, who did not think of the marvel as a possible source of entertainment nor as a tool of learning. There was no yardstick by which they could gauge the potential of this thing that was developed by so many and brought to the foreground by so few.

The introduction of television in the early 1900's could have transfigured events of history and born strongly on the actions of world figures. Could lightning-fast communication by picture have prevented World War I or de-emphasized World War II? Would the oratory gymnastics of a Hitler have reduced his thumping fists and stiff posturing to the level of low, comic burlesque? Would Franklin D. Roosevelt's propaganda "fireside chats" have been as effective with his acerbic countenance in view?

In 1816, a lonely Swedish chemist, Baron Jons Jakob Berzelius, came across a visual phenomenon in his laboratory during some geology studies that caused him joy as well as consternation. In experimenting with iron ore, he isolated an element that possessed a peculiar property: the speck of matter gave off a small degree of electricity when subjected to the ordinary light from a window. When placed in the sunlight, the electrical charge grew—it varied and reacted to light; when placed in the dark, the matter glowed, somewhat like the moon. Berzelius, brilliant, but unimaginative, christened the element selenium (meaning moon in Greek).

Berzelius had discovered the photoelectric effect in which electrons are released from a substance by light. He did not realize the importance of his discovery because the electron—that tiniest part of the atom—would not be discovered until 1891. The chemist had actually found a source of illumination which was the first step in creating something upon which an object could be reproduced: his discovery would lead to the eyes of television—the television screen itself.

Only an interesting phenomenon, selenium remained unused for some fifty years. In the meantime Royal E. House of Vermont patented an interesting device by which an operator could type out a message on a keyboard in one area, and the message would be typed out automatically at the other end of a circuit in another area: the first tele-typewriter system. This was the popular beginning of circuitry, that complex system without which all great communications discoveries would have never taken place, from the beginnings of television to the computations by our moon astronauts.

During the American Civil War yet another plateau was reached. In Amiens, France, the Abbé Caselli sent a drawing through a wire to Paris. By what matter of means a *religieux* was able to achieve this feat has not been left to us, but his accomplishment was surely no mere act of faith. So, thus far, science knew about illumination, circuitry, and a series of dots that made a crude picture; these elements were not yet brought together but they were there—in separate parts of the world.

The so-called art of communication was steadily growing by 1886 when the last section of the Trans-Atlantic cable was finally completed. This dramatic achievement, which many learned men said would never come about, was the capstone of that era.

The windswept Trans-Atlantic station at Valentia, Ireland, was the scene of the next pertinent advancement for television science when an inquisitive cable operator, named May, seeking to discover the source of static trouble in the cable, took a section apart and found that one of the bars, used as a resistor in a circuit, acted strangely under certain conditions. These bars reacted to light. He had discovered all over again the same conditions that had intrigued Berzelius so much. The bars were, of course, selenium and they were glowing and giving off electricity.

May built a wooden box with a sliding door and placed the crystalline selenium bars inside. When the door of the box was closed, the bars remained fused with very little light, but when the door was opened their conductivity increased from fifteen to one hundred percent! May was overcome by his discovery, but he lacked the mental brilliance and the scientific tools to build a machine to transmit pictures electrically, although, in his quiet way, he realized the great possibilities of selenium as a conducting agent.

Two years later, in 1875, G. R. Carey, a rather staid Bostonian, designed the world's first television set. Carey had always been intrigued with the human eye. If the eye can see, he reasoned, why could not a facsimile of the eye be built that would also see? He decided to recreate the human eye scientifically with man-made materials.

Carey knew from research that the glow from a single sheet of selenium was not sufficient to reproduce a picture, so he crumpled the element into small pieces which he affixed to a square—hoping that each cell would create a little light field of its own, increasing the total illumination. He called this square of tiny cells a "mosaic." Then he made a bank of lights with exactly as many bulbs as there were pieces of selenium in the mosaic, and he attached a separate wire from each bulb to its corresponding selenium cell. In the back of the mosaic he placed a lens, and in back of the lens he placed the object he wished to reproduce (let us say, for example, the figure "8") painted in black on a white background.

Carey's taciturn New England background must have allowed at least one whoop of joy because his system worked. The black figure "8" did not noticeably react on the selenium cells, but the entire white area surrounding the figure did react. The selenium cells glowed, sending a small current over to the bank of lights, all of which lighted up except the dark area of the figure which was crudely visible.

This, then, was the actual beginning of television. But, Carey could go no further, because he needed a booster or amplifier which Dr. Lee de Forest, the father of radio, would not present to the world until 1906 when he brought forth the three-element radio tube (fashioned out of a tiny electric light from a Christmas tree and a small piece of wire). This amplifier would be capable of intensifying electric impulses thousands of times. Carey's main contribution, then, was breaking selenium into a mosaic—the same kind of mosaic which covers the face of our television picture tube today although the sluggish selenium has long since been replaced with a radiant cesium-silver compound.

The next important revelation is attributed to Dr. Paul Nipkow, who noticed that in reading the human eye travels over the first line from left to right, then automatically returns to the second line, then the third, et cetera. He reasoned that pictures could probably be *sent* by a similar method of scanning. He placed eighteen holes, or apertures, in a metal disc. As a light flashed on the oval, which rotated, the outermost apertures traced a line across the top of the image, and this light varied according to the lights and shadows on the image being projected. When this outermost aperture had passed over the image, the next inner aperture traced out the next line, immediately below the line just scanned. The disc revolved only eighteen times a second (one second for each aperture) and each aperture traced only one line.

The completed picture, made up of eighteen lines, was shadowy and unreal and flickered badly. There was little definition, but you could discern an image. However, in order for Nipkow's disc to send out detailed pictures, he would have had to have made many more apertures in the metal oval and to find a stronger power source than electricity, which could only move the disc eighteen times per second.

Today, in order for our television set to present us with the superb reception which we all expect, pictures must be sent out via six million electric impulses a second; only electrons can move that fast without the eye detecting the magic at work.

By 1907, with Carey's mosaic principle, Nipkow's disc, Alexander Graham Bell's telephone, Heinrich Hertz's radio waves, Marconi's wireless, and Einstein's theory of the photoelectric effect—which defined the way in which a camera could turn a picture into electricity—television was almost a practical science, but it still belonged in the laboratory. Scientists in that year looked expectantly to Russia, where physicist Boris Rosing in St. Petersburg patented a television system which featured an electronic receiver that resembles the ones in use today. Dr. Rosing placed Carey's mosaic on the inside surface of a tube, but a special kind of tube called the cathode ray which K. F. Braun had perfected in 1897. But Rosing ran into the same familiar problem that had confounded his cohorts—the weak signal needed a booster and de Forest's radio tube amplifier was still in its infancy. In truth, even de Forest didn't know to what capacity his amplifier could perform; it was mainly used to strengthen radio signals.

There was still a great deal of research needed on transmission and reception, and in 1908, A. A. Campbell-Swinton, an English scientist, having been taught that everything in the universe must possess law and order, reasoned that if the cathode ray tube could work on the receiving end of television, then it would probably work equally well on the transmitting end. It could act as a kind of camera. Campbell-Swinton took three years more to research his theory before he presented the schematic for a patent and made his announcement to the world. But the project was ill-timed.

Many scientists were now bored with the idea of a complicated futuristic tube system of communications. The industrial revolution was still bringing chaos to big companies forced into retooling; automobiles were replacing horses, and money from government and industry was fluctuating wildly with the airing about of many new schemes. A carpetbagger reaction was setting in. The United States Supreme Court frowned on corporate interests and ordered Standard Oil and American Tobacco to dissolve. Woodrow Wilson was elected president and trouble was brewing abroad. Television research, at last on the very brink of making an important breakthrough, floundered. There was no important money backing the project. Most of the men who had thus far contributed to the medium had used their own money, and many had never financially recovered.

Then, too, the populace had been treated to a number of other almost incomprehensible inventions in the last few years that had left them troubled and suspicious. That new-fangled contraption, the telephone, was still regarded by many uneducated persons as an "instrument of evil" to be avoided at all costs, and even the telegraph was suspect: didn't death messages always arrive by wire? Even "having their picture took" frightened many well-intentioned people. If television had been introduced at that time in America without a sufficient period of mass education a certain strata might have regarded the wonder as a kind of sorcery. How could one live in New York and look at a picture of someone taken at that same moment in Miami? Just a few years earlier, audiences ran screaming out of nickelodeons showing *The Great Train Robbery* when the hero had fired a gun point blank at the audience!

However, in the next year a catastrophic event occurred that changed the public's mind about one medium of communication—the wireless. On an April afternoon in 1912, an obscure telegrapher named David Sarnoff, employed by Wanamakers' Department Store in New York to man wireless equipment used for advertising, sat bored and restless at his instruments. Suddenly, he took notice. Over the earphones came the first distress signals from the *Titanic*, which was sinking fast, having struck an iceberg. Immediately young Sarnoff started to alert ships in the area, and he kept at his key for seventy-two hours straight, keeping the world informed of the disaster.

Public reaction was immediate: equip more ships with this wonderful instrument so that other disasters could be avoided. Typically, it had taken a shattering new event to awaken the masses to the possibilities of communication. But there was nothing so stupendous as the sinking of the *Titanic* to unleash the wonders of television.

The United States government looked briefly at the tons of research connected with the medium, and unearthed sounding devices to detect submarines and enemy ships when World War I was finally declared in 1914. Wireless radio during the constant battles was used more and more to acquaint the public with the world crises, but its great heyday would not come until after the hostilities. Meanwhile new names hit the airwaves: Marne, Ypres, Verdun, Somme, and Cambrai.

After the peace treaty was signed at Versailles, the communications world again turned to television, but radio had gotten there first and would reach its golden age in the next decade, making household words of the names of Ruth Etting, Paul Whiteman, Kate Smith, Amos 'n Andy, and a host of others. Four hundred thousand sets were in use in 1922 when the first commercial broadcast was sent out over WEAF in New York City.

After the war, John Logie Baird of England made great technical progress with his own television system, using a Nipkow disc and mechanical cameras. He did not make use of electronics. Dr. Vladimir Zworykin had left Russia for the United States and patented his Iconoscope camera tube in 1925, revolutionizing television research thus far, for it harnessed electrons in a sophisticated manner. The tube was a great refinement over the cathode ray tube of Campbell-Swinton.

If television had been placed on the market at this time, would the twenties, that great era of emancipation, have produced such a roar? Would the flapper and the sheik have been quite so flamboyant at home watching the small tube in the living room instead of rushing to the nearest speakeasy for more salubrious entertainment?

With education progressing at such a high rate, had television been unleased upon the masses then, the maturation age of children could have advanced to such a degree that it would have been entirely possible that the chaotic conditions of the twenties and thirties could have been lessened by the time those youngsters had reached adulthood. For instance, Dr. Margaret Mead, the anthropologist, has said: "When the outside world came into the home only through reading, parents could protect their children until they learned to read, and even later to some extent, by selecting what reading matter was brought into the home or borrowed from the public library. When radio arrived, the outside world entered earlier, when children were about four. And American children now meet the pressures of the world teeming with conflict and contrast, with the vividness of television, by the age of two."

During the twenties, when several corporations decided to invest money in television research, it was not an altogether altruistic trend. Only when big business saw indications on the horizon that looked like pure gold was money made available by grants and contributions to bring about formal research programs.

Some farsighted film makers, however, realized that television really belonged to the area of communications. In Germany, in 1925, pioneer director Fritz Lang used a television screen for the first time in his classic film *Metropolis*, a striking and meaningful foray into modern times. Lang used a background projection technique to show pictures on his television screen. By the thirties a television set was quite a commonplace instrument in many science fiction movies. Ming the Merciless kept Flash Gordon under almost constant surveillance in all those serials with the type of screen device which we now know as closed circuit television. But in films, no one ever sat down to watch a ball game, a ballet, or a stage play.

In fact, even the inventors themselves did not envision television as an entertainment or education force. Certainly few persons thought that television would become competition for motion pictures, live sports events, or cultural programs. Who would sit hours on end watching something happening at some remote part of the country?

Meanwhile, Baird in England had succeeded in sending the picture of a woman all the way from London to Harsdale, New York, in 1928 and, a little later the same year, televised the world's first picture in color. It had long been known that color itself would be no problem, once the logistics had been worked out for black and white reception.

The lists of persons promoting various television systems at this time were many and varied: Philo T. Farnsworth in California, Dr. Ernst F. Alexanderson of General Electric, Dr. Herbert Ives of Bell Laboratories, which had just pioneered sound with Warner Brothers Studios and, of course, Zworykin was continuing his research on electronic camera tubes. Although the definition of televised pictures was improving rapidly, sound was still detached from the picture, and located in a separate cabinet. The sound box was called *audio* and the TV set *video;* both were transmitted by separate wave lengths. (It would be 1938 before Zworykin patented a system for broadcasting both pictures and sound on the same frequency.)

Television used the same channels assigned to radio broadcasting, so any transmission had to take place after the networks went off the air, usually at midnight.

Baird's English system was still purely electrical, the cameras were mechanical, and the scanning disc was large and unwieldly. The equipment (as were others of the period) was extremely cumbersome and unsightly—far from the compact models of today. However, the

237

disc did have thirty apertures and was able to send out thirty pictures a second and therefore avoid flicker. Baird's biggest problem was illumination; while stark white and pure black were clearly visible on the TV screen, there were no in between shades of grey and detail was almost nonexistent. One had to view the set in an almost totally dark room. But Baird's system was the best that England had to offer, and what it lacked in mobility was more than compensated with the imaginative use of ingenious programming.

In 1929, Bell Telephone tested a color television system and the ever busy Zworykin introduced a Kinetoscope cathode ray receiving set. When the stock market trembled and then finally hit bottom, the wise men of science shook their heads; surely research money would be cut off with the country facing a great depression. Strangely, just the opposite was true! Many new concerns entered the field admittedly more engaged with promoting the new wonder than rendering research, but the money added to the enormous investments already made by the old standby companies created a lot of national publicity. Jenkins, de Forest, Don Lee, DuMont, CBS, NBC, Sanabria, Westinghouse, Philco, Farnsworth, General Electric, and Bell Labs were some of the names linked with the new medium at that time. But Radio Corporation of America was still the biggest sole contributor of time, effort, and money and RCA's first telecast in 1930 featured the popular comic strip character, Felix the Cat.

Television, though, was not ready yet for the big push. Too many problems needed to be solved, too many questions remained unanswered. Sets, if marketed, would cost several thousands of dollars at a time when two dollars a day was considered a fair wage for a laborer. Transmitting wave lengths had not yet been assigned, nor television studios set up for programs, and no governing body had been formed to police the new medium. Who would *pay* to place programs on the air? In short, a big promotional push had been created in the hope of providing a miracle that would arrest hard times. With no revenue likely to come in for a decade, one by one, the companies retrenched and the miracle fuse was smudged out. Commercial television was a long dream away.

But questions, larger than life, intrigued the thinkers, those men in the industry, like Sarnoff, who were always ready to make a public statement at the drop of a hat. Prophets that they were, there was still no way of foretelling how to send a picture from one area to another when stations were able to transmit only within a fifty mile area. Cables could perhaps carry the signal, but who would absorb the cost of connecting every hamlet in America? Bell Telephone might be persuaded to cooperate. Nevertheless, when the cables were laid exactly what would television show? Microwave stations that dotted the country as relay points were twenty years in the future, and programming was only a word in the dictionary.

As the thirties wore on, and the nation's economy dipped lower and lower, England, her pound sterling on an even keel, was making good strides, not only in television research but telecasting techniques as well, but Baird's system was barred in February, 1937, with the BBC's decision to use the Marconi system exclusively. This was a bitter blow to John Logie Baird, who had contributed so much to making television a practical possibility. That he failed to use an electronic instead of a purely mechanical system was his only mistake, but it cost him his dream of establishing a Baird system all over Continental Europe. Meanwhile, Sweden, Germany, and Japan were going ahead with their own systems (many patterned after Baird's) under a "closed door" policy—let the Americans use electronic tubes with exclusive patents!

The BBC, notwithstanding, was telecasting lively events; the February, 1937, broadcast from the Alexandra Palace had a fifty mile range, but was only a test for the George VI coronation later in the month, which was a magnificent spectacle for the few people who owned sets. Although the London telecasts were short-range, an occasional program was picked up as far away as Riverhead, New York, because of unsettled atmospheric conditions. This was possible because television was still using radio frequencies.

In that same year, Gilbert Seldes was appointed head of the CBS TV program department in New York. He tried his best to assemble some sort of creative visual material instead of relying upon cold factual demonstrations put on by engineers of other networks and TV equipment manufacturers.

NBC had some success in televising a scene from the Broadway hit *Susan and God*, with Gertrude Lawrence, and Sanabria showed an excerpt from another play in a film theatre on a screen measuring twenty feet by fifteen. This test was the forerunner of the "big screen TV" which brings to us the championship fights, the Indianapolis 500, and other sports events viewed in theatres with portable equipment.

Many sets at this time were large cabinets reminiscent of the old-style four foot high Victrolas, featuring a "flip top" lid containing a mirror that raised to a slanting position. The picture came over the tube upside down and was reversed and then reflected in the mirror. Truthfully, reception left something to be desired. The definition was poor, the image often distorted, or covered with "snow," and the picture sometimes flipped over to break in to varied patterns, somewhat reminiscent of a monochrome kaleidoscope.

Only RCA stayed in the industry in a big way, confident that when Zworykin came out with his new Iconoscope electronic camera, all other similar equipment would be obsolete. They were right, for the Iconoscope was hailed as the electronic wonder—the big breakthrough for which engineers had been waiting. Now, the scanning discs with their shadowy, ill-defined pictures and the cumbersome, mechanical cameras were truly passé. The Iconoscope stabilized the unsteady world of television.

The brilliant Russians, like Carey and Campbell-Swinton, went back to the human eye for the Iconoscope, which duplicated the functions of the eye as no other device ever had before. The new tube began with a mosaic of a thin sheet of mica, upon which had been implanted microscopic globules of sensitized cesium-silver compound. Microscopically separate, these globules were placed on the mica in such a way that they did not come in contact with one another—each formed an individual plate, and when hit by light, emitted electrons in proportion to the amount of light that hit each one. Therefore, a light background picture exuded more light, a face considerably less, while a dress or a tree or a curtain transmitted as different shades of grey, which were picked up in relative value by each one of those thousands of dots on the mosaic television screen. These globules today are no more apparent—even under close inspection—than the minute dots that make up a halftone photograph in a magazine.

A different type of scanning was perfected making sophisticated use of the "electronic gun," which, complicated and fascinating, brought a full array of grey shading and finite definition to the picture tube.

The electron gun, located in the throat of the tube, simply shoots a stream of electrons toward the mosaic, performing this action in an extremely orderly manner. Aimed first at the top of the mosaic, it scans the first line (just as we scan when we read), then it whips back and scans the third line, then the fifth. When it reaches the bottom of the plate, it reverts back to the top of the plate and "reads" the alternate lines, second, fourth, sixth, et cetera, it missed before. Each process of scanning the odd and even lines takes only one sixtieth of a second (added together to bring the total to one-thirtieth of a second) which sends out thirty pictures, one after the other.

The electron gun reads a line thirty thousand times quicker than the fastest human reader in the world, so it is not apparent that the above operation is taking place at all. Because of persistence of vision, we only see a smooth continuous movement. The screen, made up of 525 lines, half of which are scanned the first time, and half the second time, provides a beautifully detailed picture.

From a purely artistic standpoint, the Iconoscope of the thirties had several inherent faults. The high amount of hot light needed for the camera was so enormous that personalities being televised were extremely uncomfortable. The lights were so intense the features were often wiped out. The famous Hollywood makeup expert, Max Factor, was asked to create a special makeup, a dead-white compound that harked back to the days of silent pictures. But even then, performers were often blurred by electronic tricks. To combat this problem, Factor later devised the "painted Indian" look in 1936.

This bizarre makeup has long since faded from the scene. For the last thirteen years, since the more sensitive Image Orthicon tube, all that is needed for male television makeup is a light facial base, while females need only add the usual extras, such as eyebrow pencil and lipstick.

Gilbert Seldes has said about those hectic days of 1939 when the world was being tuned for war: ". . . there were no sponsors, no commercials, and almost no money for talent. We [CBS] paid $250.00 for the rights to Faulkner's lovely story, 'Two Soldiers,' and the cost for the half-hour dramatization we made must have run to $500.00."

The Fifth Avenue Easter Parade was telecast in New York in 1939 and later in the month, the much heralded television coverage of the New York World's Fair. According to the *New York Times,* which covered the event, the telecast opened at 12:30 P.M. on April 30 with a long shot view of the trylon and perisphere; the camera then panned the crowds, the fountains, and the waving flags near the Court of Peace where the opening ceremonies were about to begin. Mrs. James Roosevelt sat beside the First Lady on the dais, followed by Mrs. Woodrow Wilson, Frances Perkins (Secretary of Labor), James A. Farley (Postmaster General), Mr. and Mrs. William Bankhead (Speaker of the House), Mr. and Mrs. William Woodring (Secretary of War), Henry Wallace (Secretary of Agriculture), and Frank Murphy (Secretary General), along with Mayor La Guardia, Governor Lehman, and Grover A Whalen. President Roosevelt's car entered the grounds and a short while later he was on camera.

It was certainly a sedate scene, an occasion of dignity. Eleanor Roosevelt, conscious of the television equipment, would not have dreamed that she would find television, in her old age, a way by which elderly people could live happily, endlessly entertained. President Roosevelt himself, facing the battery of microphones and the TV camera, would have been greatly impressed to know that another Democrat would later win an election mainly because he came over so vibrantly and at ease on the home tube. John Kennedy, before he went to the White House, knew the importance of the electronic magic lantern: "The wonders of science and technology have revolutionized the modern political campaign. . . . But nothing compares to the revolutionary impact of television. TV has altered drastically the nature of our campaigns, conventions, constituents, candidates and costs."

Times correspondent Orrin E. Dunlap, Jr. noted that, "Of all the notables viewed, Mayor La Guardia is the most telegenic. . . ."

Reception was marred only by a few white streaks, thought to be caused by switching operations. Unfortunately, the historic telecast was viewed on only about two hundred sets, including those studio monitors scattered about Greater New York.

The only criticism of the affair was voiced by the admittedly more technically advanced British engineers, who churlishly suggested that the Americans had nerve using only one camera when they would have used three or four and showed the festivities from different angles. What would have happened, they peevishly asked, if the electric eye had gone out? One of the American engineers replied philosophically, "That's not our luck, but should the 'electric eye' go blind, then we are licked." Actually NBC had only two cameras, and was lucky to spare one for the World's Fair telecast.

The next day, television sets went on sale in New York stores, advertised from $200.00 (an attachable unit to coincide with radio receivers) up to $2,000.00 (a full scale model with a "big" 15 inch screen).

On March 5, 1939, with the publicity of the fair's telecast still ringing in his ears, David Sarnoff made another far-reaching prophecy that no one understood even vaguely: "The means are at hand," he said, "for a new era in human relationships. . . . If a hurricane marches up our coasts we are warned to prepare for it long before it arrives; will we someday watch its progress beyond the horizon?" Sarnoff, paterfamilias of television, was, of course, alluding to the present-day satellites that roam our skies like vigilant watchdogs.

The BBC suspended TV service on September 17 because of the war. The Federal Communications Commission, with an eye to world crisis, conducted a public hearing on January 15, 1940, and issued several statements. For instance, the report stipulated RCA spent ten billion dollars on research from 1934 to 1939 while CBS spent one million per year and no telecasts were regularly scheduled.

By March, RCA decided to lower the cost of sets to about $395.00 which prompted the FCC to take action. The public, was the decree, should understand that television was still experimental—a set bought at that time would not be fully operable for a long time to come, nor should viewers expect to receive a wide variety of programs.

What was actually troubling the FCC, of course, was that channels had not yet been assigned to the networks. Sets would be tuned to the existing transmitters. When the wave lengths were changed, the sets in operation would be no longer usable, since it would cost a prohibitive amount of money to return them to the factory for rebuilding. (It was much the same situation that came about over color television fifteen years later. CBS had a remarkable color system brought out under the guidance of Peter Goodmark, which had received FCC approval. RCA also had a color system still undergoing tests. When the FCC discovered that the CBS system was not compatible with sets already in existence, that is to say, color shows could not be picked up in black and white, the Commission reversed itself and gave RCA the "go ahead" because their system was compatible—allowing color transmission to be picked up on existing monochrome sets.)

After Europe was plunged into war and the television facilities of England, Germany, France, Sweden, Italy, Poland, Russia, Holland, and Japan were shut down, it was thought that television might be an excellent reconnaissance weapon. Television could already see through fog or at night by the use of infrared rays. As early as 1938 a patent had been granted to L. J.

David Sarnoff, an obscure telegrapher, became the leading pioneer of television.

Kemp for RCA on a system for the blind landings of planes—which later, of course, became operational radar. Also, airplane pilots had watched shows from a New York studio while aloft. American television, at last on the brink of leaving the restricting abyss of experimentation and entering the affluent sphere of commercialism, closed its electric eye on December 7, 1941. The theory of peaceful television became the graffiti of battle.

After the war, the production of TV sets was stepped up and proper high frequency channels were set up for exclusive television use. TV could now broadcast all day and more of the night, and it was ironic that now that all that extra time existed—so little of it could be filled. When RCA brought out the Image Orthicon tube in 1946, the sale of sets rose because reception was excellent and the picture was well defined, sharp, clear, and infallibly honest. Honest because it was next to impossible to be dishonest on television, particularly in a talk show, since the eye of the electronic camera seemed destined to bore into the very vitals of a performer and reveal any insecurity that might lurk in his subconscious. Insecurity, pretention, vagueness, were all exposed over the tube and sometimes enlarged a hundred fold.

Audience participation shows, such as the tearful "Queen For A Day," the hilarious "I Love Lucy," the effervescent "What's My Line," and the sparkling Steve Allen "Tonight Show" were deserved hits. Television sets were still a curiosity, and neighbors who had never spoken became close friends when one possessed a set and the other did not. Tavern and bar business soared, with "TV INSIDE" plastered in huge letters on the front.

People as never before—even during the depression —began to stay home to watch television and the movie-going public dwindled. At Hollywood's darkest hour, the motion picture studios, fighting for their very existence, started to sell backlogs of old films to the new medium for much needed cash. "Who wants to see those old things!" the studio heads sniffed, pocketing the millions. But soon they were startled to discover that whole generations of young people had never seen Jean Harlow, Joan Crawford, Clark Gable, Bette Davis, John Wayne, James Stewart, Errol Flynn.

Television had revived the brilliant youth of the super-stars, who were now (with the exception of a few) in the nadir of their careers. In many cases, "box-office poison" stars made startling movie comebacks through this renewed TV exposure. Hollywood had sold itself down the river by making available these giant film backlogs to TV. Years and years of innovation and novelty, including wide-screen, stereophonic sound and even the classification of films on an adult level, would be required to woo patrons back to motion pictures.

Meanwhile, mama and papa and the kids stayed home to watch Wally Cox as "Mr. Peepers," Ethel Waters as "Beulah," "Private Secretary" with Ann Sothern, Eve Arden as "Our Miss Brooks," "Howdy Doody," "Kukla, Fran and Ollie," "Amos 'n Andy," the "Dave Garroway Show," Imogene Coca and Sid Caesar in "The Show of Shows," "The Ed Sullivan Show," "Topper," "Dagmar," "George Gobel"—and the famous soap operas which had left radio for the small screen.

In between times, families were often treated to the fun-and-games of live commercials where anything might happen. Betty Furness became famous overnight when the door of a refrigerator refused to open, leaving Miss Furness with a deep layer of egg on her face. Her employer had a famous slogan: "You can be sure—if it's Westinghouse." Bottles that refused to open on cue, animals that misbehaved, salesmen who inadvertently dented the fenders of cars, wrist watches with cracked crystals after a test, cigarettes that caused the announcer to cough . . . the possibilities were endless.

After the first act of a play dealing with Germany's annihilation camps a commercial extolled the virtues of cooking with gas! Then too, famous actors familiar with long rehearsals or many film retakes were often overcome with fear at the prospect of live television. Dame Judith Anderson, during a production of a *whodunnit* on "Climax" lost many a line and was even heard to mutter "Oh, damn" in those famous august tones. And two-time Academy Award winner Paul Muni, impersonating a famous lawyer, fiddled marvelously with a hearing aid during the long courtroom harangues and was much praised for his performance. Not revealed until much later was the fact that Muni, unable to remember lines, was outfited with a one-way radio disguised to look like a hearing aid. All that marvelous business occurred whenever the celebrated actor was forced to adjust the contraption to get his lines straight.

Youngsters were impressed most of all by TV. According to UPI reporter Robert Musel, even Queen Elizabeth clamped down on her children when they were small because Prince Charles began to sound more like the marshal of Dodge City than the heir to the ancient throne of Great Britain. Television has also changed the reading habits of the small fry. One librarian reported that a child asked for *Cinderella* by Rodgers and Hammerstein, and could not be convinced that the original was written by Charles Perrault. This incident obviously occurred after the celebrated TV musical version of the fairy tale.

To grow into adulthood in a halcyon day before electrons invade privacy is possible now only in a few out-of-the-way places: perhaps in an Africa no longer dark; on certain islands where natives still wear the sarong; in mountain areas like the Alps which defy transmission; or perhaps in some of the cold, vast, frozen wastelands of the world.

It is only a short matter of time now before satellites will carry TV signals all over the globe and cables and micro-wave relay stations will be as dead as Nipkow's disc. When this comes about, a little auxiliary box—a kind of instant translator or scramble system—will enable the nomads of Central Asia, the native of the Archipelagoes, the mountaineer and his goats, and the proud Africans to appreciate the antics of Lucy, the double entendres of Rowan and Martin, the slapstick of the Banana Splits and the exploits of the Mission Impossible gang. Truly, then, the world will be bombarded with electrons and privacy of any kind will no longer be possible.

What will then be the new "electronic magic lantern" of tomorrow? Projecting pictures out of the air on an ordinary windowpane? Transmission of a voice through the ether from a disc no bigger than a dime? Or will time stand still, and through an even greater discovery, we will hear the Sermon on the Mount—the voice of Christ chanting through two thousand years? Will we benefit from the wisdom of Socrates, share the library of Alexander the Great, accompany Cleopatra on her barge down the Nile, hear the voices of Caruso and Patti, share the drama of Michaelangelo painting the Sistine Chapel? All events are, say the scientists, imprisoned somewhere in the void of outer space. It is there to be found just like the electron opened the magic doors of television.

CONTRIBUTORS

Sam Elkin, the author of several books of history, lives in River Edge, New Jersey. Gerald Carson's books include *The Polite Americans; The Old Country Store; One For a Man, Two For a Horse,* and *The Social History of Bourbon.*

Thomas W. McKern is professor of anthropology at the University of Kansas. Sharon (Mrs. Thomas W.) McKern is a free-lance writer specializing in physical anthropology. They are co-authors of *Human Origins.* Bruce C. Williams, a free-lance writer who lives in Mill Valley, California, is a graduate of the University of Washington.

Dr. Albert G. Hess, the former director of the International and Project Services, National Council on Crime and Delinquency, is a professor of sociology at the State University of New York, Brockport, New York. William Baker is a practicing optometrist and editor of the *Oregon State Journal of Optometry.*

Brenda Gourgey has published in *History Today, Mankind, Geographical Magazine* and many other journals. She lives in Stanmore, Middlesex, England. Howald Bailey, a graduate of the University of Virginia, is a public relations consultant and free-lance writer.

Elenor L. Schoen is a free-lance writer specializing in French and English history. Richard Merrill has written articles on art history for a variety of publications.

Ronald Leal, a graduate of the University of Mexico, publishes articles on social history as well as papers on Mexico and the American Southwest. Walter Jarrett is a free-lance writer living in Los Angeles.

Robert McCarter is a former associate editor of *Mankind.* He now lives in Los Angeles and is working on a novel. Dr. Rudolph Brasch is the author of the book, *How Did Sports Begin?* He lives in Vaucluse, N.S.W., Australia.

Whitney Stine is a free-lance writer who lives in Los Angeles. He specializes in the history of communications.

Each new issue of Mankind magazine brings you the delight of discovering fresh, bold, unexpected ideas relating to man's adventure on earth. You may join the Knights Templars crusading to free the Holy Land in one article, then thrill to Lord Byron's vision of the glory that was Greece in another. You could visit with Catherine the Great of Russia, travel in the western badlands with Jesse James, explore the London slums of Hogarth's England or battle with Grant at Vicksburg. The writing is lively. The subjects fascinating. The format bold and dynamic. Priceless photographs, authentic maps and drawings and magnificent art in full color illustrate articles written by the world's foremost historians and authors. Mankind is the most entertaining and rewarding magazine you and your family can read. Discover the pleasure of reading Mankind now. Your introductory subscription rate is only $5 for the full 6-issue year.